Heard Mentality

An A-Z Guide to Taking Your Podcast or Radio Show from Idea to Hit

Celeste Headlee
Edited by Don Smith

With contributions from:

Jamila Bey
Cindy Carpien
Alex Cohen
Jeff Hansen
Steve Inskeep
Jay Kernis
Al Letson
Michel Martin
Rachel Martin
Ellen McDonnell
Irene Noguchi
Susan Stamberg
Carline Watson

CONTENTS

FIRST THINGS FIRST (AN INTRODUCTION)

If you want to launch an audio show of any kind, even a podcast, you've come to the right place. This book offers a combined 400 years or so of experience in broadcasting. If there's a mistake to be made, we've probably made it, and I'd love to warn you about it so you don't make it, too.

This is real-world, practical, honest advice. I just want you to be as informed and prepared as possible so you can create an inspiring program. This is intended to cover your show's first three years of broadcasting and I've divided it into specific categories so you can easily consult the section you need as issues arise.

I've launched many new shows over the course of my career. Creating a new show out of nothing is perhaps the hardest task I've ever faced. And yet, it's incredibly rewarding when it's done right. Imagine how it would feel to say, "I helped create *This American Life* or *Radiolab* or *Serial*." There is nothing else in broadcasting quite like creating something from nothing, to overcome the obstacles, and solve each problem, until you have something listeners value. The first time you hear someone say, "I love your show! I listen every day!," you'll know all your hard work was worthwhile.

It's true listeners have a lot of options, but many of them are terrible. Excellent broadcasts are few and far between. Most cities don't have a lot of high quality news options or arts and cultural coverage. So if you're careful in crafting your show, in responding to listener needs, and in choosing the right team, you can create something people will rely on and cherish.

I'm here to help you do that, but first...

Maybe you shouldn't do this - Celeste Headlee

Before you take a single step toward launching a talk show, newsmagazine or podcast, ask yourself, "Is this a good idea? No, seriously, am I sure this is necessary?"

There are a lot of shows out there (including podcasts) that don't need to exist. The audience doesn't want them. They're often motivated more by the creator's desire to make a podcast than by a need in the community. A new show is very expensive (at least $500,000 annually, on average) and extremely labor-intensive (5-7 staff members working full-time for a daily one-hour show). It will most likely take years to become successful, if it ever does.

That's why it's vital you make sure you're launching a show for the right reasons and you have the resources (read: money) to do this right. Don't make the mistake of assuming you can hire a producer, put the host and a guest in front of a mic, and make the case to your listeners that it's worth supporting because it's local.

As Ellen McDonnell, NPR's former Executive Editor for News, says, "If you can't produce a first-rate show that's compelling, reflects the community, and serves the audience, why are you bothering? It can't be a vanity show. It has to cut through all the other stuff that's out there."

It's essential to do some audience research before creating a new local show. What is in the data that shows the audience wants your show? Are they listening to commercial radio instead of your content? Does your existing audience want more talk radio? And if listeners do want a local show, what's the best time for it? Look at your format and ask, "Why do we really want to do this?" What are you trying to accomplish with your show? You should craft a mission statement and, to a certain extent, your success should be measurable.

Podcasts are available all over the globe, but a local radio show is grounded in a specific place. Before you start to create a great local show, make sure you're clear on what your station really wants and needs. According to a 2015 study, it costs more to produce an hour of local content than to buy it from a network. And listeners may punish you if you take away high-quality network programming and replace it with mediocre local content. Public radio consultant John Sutton writes in *Current* that public radio listeners "consider themselves citizens of the world. The geographic constraints on a local station's content creators cannot fulfill the listeners' full range of interests. The absence of national and international content will drive listeners away."

The number of local talk and interview shows in public radio plummeted by almost 40% between 2007 and 2015. That's because it's all about return on investment and serving the listeners, not about being able to say that you produce your own show. Research tells us audiences prefer a good national show over a mediocre local one.

I can almost hear your thinking, "She's talking about someone else. We can do it and do it well, and listeners will appreciate it." You might be right, but statistically speaking, you probably aren't. The fact is, most stations don't have enough staff to produce a high quality local show. Sutton found that only 20 of the 62 local shows he studied were adequately staffed. He says, "Often there are more people working on digital components than on the broadcast itself." About 20 other shows are "doing the best they can with limited resources." They have only three or four people on staff and one of those is responsible for updating the website and social media.

The rest of those local shows, 22 or so, have only a handful of people on staff. That's simply not enough to make quality content, plus maintain an online presence. I wish I could be kinder and gentler about saying this, but it's important to make this point: mediocre local content costs more and does less. So, consider carefully before you spend money on a show that doesn't serve your audience or help your station grow.

Now that I've got that out of the way…

Let's consider the hard stuff.

STEP ONE: FIND THE RIGHT HOST

Here's why it's so difficult to find a great host: the most essential skills can't be taught.

It pains me to write that sentence and it will hurt some of you to read it. I started this book under the opposite impression. I wanted to figure out how to train hosts. I wanted to develop a reliable method of training a reporter or *Morning Edition* anchor to be a truly great talk show host. As it turns out, it can't be done unless the raw talent is already there. You can't start from zero.

The challenge is not how to train *anyone* to be a host, but how to recognize the talent and potential in someone, then develop it. That's not a simple task. Many managers rely on their gut feelings when choosing a host. I don't recommend that. Your gut is often fooled, and all too easily influenced by things unrelated to the raw potential of a host. You should trust your instinct, but be conscious of the fact that it is neither totally reliable nor infallible.

The bad news is, there are intangibles in hosting that can't be listed on a job description. The good news is, the intangibles are relatively rare. Most of the skills required for hosting can be described, identified, and tested. That means you can go into the recruitment process with a list of qualities to look for and a list of the things you want to avoid.

So, here you'll find a guide not just to identifying hosts, but developing their talents and skills so they sound better in their third year than they did in their first. This is a critical part of the process.

On-air host is one of the most crucial and visible jobs at a station; yet, hosts often get the least training. Managers hire them, make sure they're on the air every day, and think their job is done. I've spoken with hosts who've anchored shows for years and never had an air check or a workshop or any kind of development opportunity. That's a recipe for bad radio, bad ratings, and an unhappy host.

Perhaps the most significant lack in developing host talent or producing a great local show is management's involvement. Make no mistake: I can't teach you how to identify talent, hire them, and then ignore them. Management needs to be involved in the entire process of creating new shows. Once they're launched, managers must continue to be involved.

There are a number of reasons for this. First, managers sometimes say their on-air talent is hard to manage. That's often because they tend to get involved only when something has gone wrong. Second, it's hard to know what resources your team needs and which requests are reasonable if you are isolated from the process. Third, it might be difficult to grow the show or change it unless you understand the producers' workflow and how the show is put together. Finally, and most importantly, you can't manage and support staff when you don't know them as people and you don't know what they do as producers. If you're not involved, you could become the kind of manager who shows up only when the staff is angry or you need to intervene in a dispute. No one wants to be that guy (or gal).

DON'T TRUST YOUR GUT

Because there are intangibles associated with great hosting (is he likeable? does she sound personable? how is his energy? is she interested in the topic?), many administrators rely on their guts for final decisions. Don't do that. Remember, your gut cannot be trusted.

This is not often discussed openly in our industry, but I would be remiss if I were less than absolutely honest about it. Have you ever wondered why so many public radio hosts and managers are white men? Most of us have spent enough time with our colleagues in the industry to know we're not surrounded by racists who think white guys are better than everyone else. I don't know a single general manager who believes white guys are more dedicated journalists, sound more credible, or appeal more to listeners than women or people of color.

So, why are white guys so over-represented among on-air talent and management? Based on my experience, it's because of people's guts.

Every human being on the planet has some implicit biases. Plus, the best research we have says we tend to like people who are similar to us. For most of us, this isn't conscious. We don't think, "I want to work with this person because he also grew up middle class, likes the music I like and the TV shows I like, and thinks the same news stories are important, and also wears Doc Martens." But those things influence your gut.

Your gut tells you this person is the right choice; you can't explain why. But your gut is swayed by all of those biases and stereotypes that we all have and must confront consciously if we are to ignore them.

Sally Lehrman, SPJ's National Diversity Chairwoman, wrote about this in her report, "News in a New America": "Because they operate at an unconscious level, stereotypes have their most power when people make subjective choices or must rely on incomplete information. Absent professional personnel practices, that's the way newsrooms tend to assign and promote, and when diversity remains unspoken and invisible except when it's time for staff counts, the ambiguity creates a lot of room for guesses and misunderstandings."

Let's say you have three candidates for a hosting job, all well qualified, equally hard working, and highly recommended. Often, the decision on which person to hire comes down to gut instinct. Most of our administrators in broadcasting are white males. And research says they will feel most comfortable with, and most likely to trust, other white males. So when they make hiring decisions, our largely white, largely male management chooses mostly white males.

This is not necessarily racism. It's natural and human, and can be traced back to survival skills that we simply haven't evolved out of or outgrown. The tendency to trust people who look like we do is instinctive, regardless of our color or gender. Since we all do it, that means we all have to be on the lookout for it.

Stop relying on your gut! It will betray you. I had to learn not to trust my instincts. I have subconscious biases, despite the fact I'm about as multicultural as someone can be. I'm still human; I still grew up making assumptions about people and those assumptions still live somewhere inside my psyche. They influence my feelings about what stories are significant and which aren't, and they make me feel a connection with some people more readily than with others.

I don't trust my gut, and you shouldn't either. The guts of some program directors and GMs and executive producers keep us from achieving real diversity in broadcasting. Get input from people who have different perspectives and experiences. You can even bring someone else in during the interview. Judge applicants with as objective an eye as possible. You can't be free of biases, but you can be aware of them.

Think very hard before hiring someone who has no experience in the job for which they've applied. Leaps of faith are usually based on giving one candidate the benefit of the doubt. Research shows managers aren't objective in who gets the benefit of the doubt. Multiple studies have shown both male and female managers are more likely to hire men for jobs in which they have no experience than to hire women with the same qualifications. We are more likely to give males the benefit of the doubt. Put your candidates through their paces, test them, and then have others listen to the results and evaluate them.

IDENTIFY TALENT

You can be trained to be a good reporter, but not a great one. A great host can't be trained. It's all about hiring the right person from the start. -Al Letson, host of Reveal

Finding a good host is not as simple as finding a smart person who can talk. It doesn't matter if you're recruiting for a radio show or a podcast, finding the right host is harder than you think.

It can depend on what's being hosted. If you're creating your own podcast, the right host may not be you. Many people may have told you: "You should be on the radio!" They may be wrong.

Talk show hosting is not the same as local hosting. Let me repeat that -- being a good talk show host requires an almost completely different set of skills than hosting *Morning Edition*. Let's establish terms first. A local anchor is someone who does the local inserts in a network show, like *Morning Edition* or *All Things Considered*. Many stations call them hosts, but a host is someone who anchors their own show. I understand there's some personal ego involved in this, but I'm being precise and straight-forward. They are two very different jobs, and really need two different titles.

It's also a mistake to think a great reporter who sounds good doing live interviews will be a strong host. NPR's Supreme Court Correspondent Nina Totenberg is a perfect example of why you can't always transplant a great reporter into a host's chair. Nina is an exceptional reporter; she would probably not be a good host. Totenberg's strengths are in writing and relaying complicated information simply. She is not a generalist like a host; she is a specialist. Her gift is not in throwing attention on someone else, but in drawing attention. And why would you want to take her out of a job at which she's outstanding and waste her talents in a completely different position?

Many hosts aren't good reporters, and they also might make pretty terrible local anchors. That's because reporter, host and local anchor are all different jobs. The parts are not interchangeable in this machine. As Alex Cohen, the host of *Take Two* at KPCC in Los Angeles, says, "You can't have a swimmer teach rugby, even if they're both athletic jobs that involve sports." A news reporter or anchor first has to relay information, not connect with the audience. Reporters give you the facts; hosts tell you a story.

Finding the right host will take time, and it will require a different method than the familiar phone interview followed by in-person interview and then reference check and job offer. Jay Kernis, NPR's former Senior V.P. of

Programming, says this is not a job interview: "Be with that person. Go to lunch. How big is your crush? It's not unlike a date. Do you want to spend time with them? She may have a great voice, great experience, but you might think, 'I don't think I like her very much.' That's a big red flag. Honestly, will your listeners like and trust this person? Hosts love other people and are empathetic and sincerely want to learn about other people."

Someone can be great in interviews and terrible on the air. They might be great in pre-recorded segments and awful live. Someone might be an incredible host in Seattle and out of tune in Los Angeles. Ideally, you need to spend several days with your candidate. You'll want to put them through their paces and form more than a first impression.

Most companies can't afford that. So, another option is to bring in your top two or three candidates for a week. A week is enough time to know if the person can listen, is passionate, is curious, and can ask good questions. Managers often let potential hosts talk to producers for 30 minutes or so, but producers need a couple days to get a read on prospects. They need to go over scripts with them, work with them in the studio, see how they get along.

Bringing them in for a week will tell you the basics about your candidate, but it's not enough time to know if he's a team player, if she can write well, if he handles pressure capably or has a good instinct for news stories. So, once you've identified a good prospect, sign your host to a one-year contract to start. If you don't make a long-term commitment, it frees you to take a risk.

WHO IS A HOST?

> *Most hosts have ego and they need it. They're going toe-to-toe with guests who also have big egos and need to respect the host. But the host also needs to be able to scale the ego back and step into the background. -Irene Noguchi, producer at KQED*

> *The word "host" is literal. That person says, "This is my house. I will make you comfortable and show you respect. - Alex Cohen, host of Take Two at KPCC*

A great host is a strong journalist, a capable writer, an engaging presence and a trustworthy personality. They pop on the air. They have a larger than life presence, with the ability to fade into the background while they shine a spotlight on someone else. Jonathan Kern describes it this way in his book, *Sound Reporting*, "They personify the network and give it voice--so that listeners rely on them when the news is fast-breaking, catastrophic or sorrowful...honest, credible, versatile, quick-witted, articulate, and indefatigable, at times tough or soothing or whimsical or funny--and always trustworthy."

A great host is extraordinarily well-read and curious. They can't be interested in only a few topics. They are renaissance people in a modern age, with insatiable curiosity. That doesn't mean they are master of any one topic. Remember, getting a PhD in education doesn't mean you're a good teacher, and a political scientist isn't always the best choice to host a political show.

An experienced host has a personality that enlivens discussion without dominating it or compromising credibility. The host manages the clock carefully and doesn't usually need time prompts from the director. They have a strong editorial sense, a deep knowledge of current topics so they can push back on guests on the fly. They have to sound conversational and be able to improvise. Things will go wrong on the air. Can your host keep her cool and maintain composure when a guest's line drops? Can he jump into existing programming with breaking news on a moment's notice, with no written script, and still sound professional and prepared?

The host's attitude toward listeners is equally important and all too often overlooked. An outstanding host has respect for the listeners. They should think, "You are choosing to give me your time, and that time is valuable. I will serve you well." Is this person respectful, in general, of others? Listeners are always judging the host, and they're looking for rude behavior. They're very sensitive to it. That means the host needs to know how to cut people off gracefully and how to break into an argument without shouting or scolding.

A host should create an engaging, relaxed conversation, while concealing all the structure and craft going on behind the scenes. Much of what happens on the air is artifice, but it can't sound like that. GPB producer Don Smith says an interview has to have a skeleton but the audience doesn't want to see the bones.

Ellen DeGeneres is so good at what she does because she seems to be effortless. She focuses attention on her guest and she seems completely delighted to talk to all of them. It can't possibly be true, but she makes it look and sound as though she would rather be talking to them than doing anything else. As NPR host Michel Martin says, "Ellen is 'just folks.' She says, 'Let me show you who I've got. Let me introduce you to my new friend.'" Michel's point? It's not about Ellen.

Alex Cohen says some of the best training for a host can be a stint as a bartender. To earn tips in that job, you have to connect, even if you don't like the customer, and it has to seem sincere. Jeff Hansen, the former Program Director at KUOW, says he avoids using the word "conversation" when talking about interviews: "The word conversation made hosts think the aim is a back-and-forth over the back fence. A great two-way sounds conversational, but it's highly structured and controlled."

A good host owns the show. They set the tone among the staff and are dedicated to excellence. They have a high emotional IQ. What is that? It's the ability to recognize their own emotions and the emotions of others. It is also an ability to manage their own emotions and help others alter their mood when that's needed.

A good host isn't afraid to reveal their own personality and perspectives. I know this makes many managers nervous, because the line between perspective and opinion is fine. But modern listeners expect more from their hosts than they did in the days of Cronkite and Sawyer. They want more than a credible authority; they want a human being, with human reactions and, occasionally, human flaws. On the Media host Brooke Gladstone says, "You don't want someone who's objective. You want someone who's fair.

The host is the surrogate for the audience. So they expect hosts to express surprise, or be arch."

Sometimes, management hires inexperienced people to save money. That's usually a mistake: hire in haste, lament at leisure. Try to hire someone who knows what they're doing. Brooke is a great example of this. *On the Media* was around for years before Brooke got there and turned the show into a success. You don't need a big name host, but you want someone with experience.

Hosting is a skill that requires practice to develop. A live host has to juggle a number of things at once: scanning emails, listening to the line producer, following news feeds, watching Twitter, listening to the guest, coming up with the next question, watching the script, listening to prompts from the director or the line producer, keeping an eye on the control room for signals from the production staff, watching the clock, cueing audio clips, and on and on. It's very important to take experience into account.

But don't make experience the final determiner. Bad host choices are sometimes made out of a fear of something new. New can embarrass you, but it can also have incredible impact. So, take the risk if it's right for you and your listeners, based on the research you've done. And if it's the wrong choice, you can recover. If CBS can get over Dan Rather, if NBC survived Brian Williams, you can get over a bad host pick, too. Just sign a limited contract, give them a chance, and then watch carefully.

Remember, all of the advice in this book is just advice: guidelines and suggestions. To be clear, they are recommendations based on about 400 years of experience in public broadcasting (that's not an exaggeration), so ignore them at your peril. Still, there are exceptions to every rule and you may find one or two. But be conscious that you are making an unusual decision and make sure it's based on sound evidence and not implicit bias.

At heart, hosting is about interviewing. The interview should be the deciding factor in choosing your host. You need to hear the host interact with guests and conduct an engaging conversation. Remember, a good interview doesn't showcase the host, but relays information to the listener. The worst hosts are those who try to make you think they're the smartest person in the room, by citing what they know about a subject or constantly telling guests what they just said. The host is the driver for the carpool who picks everyone up, knows where they're going, and gets them all there on time.

A talk show host has much more advanced and refined interviewing skills than a local host, even if the show is pre-recorded. If your host can't conduct an interview to time, you'll waste valuable time editing it. Does the interview sound like every other conversation you've heard or are the questions creative and unique? Is the host really listening to the guest and responding to what they hear? Ideally, a host should be able to conduct the interview without any prepared questions, if it's necessary. They must know how to do serious research so they're not tied to a script. Awkward moments in interviews often result from poor or no preparation by the host.

Later in the book, I'll provide a detailed guide on how to conduct an excellent two-way interview. The interview is the heart of a host's job, and they must be great at it. A strong host has a clear vision of the beginning, middle, and end of each interview before it begins. They have energy without being frenetic, good pacing, and they don't stumble for 20 seconds searching for a thought. They don't ask "filler questions." Every question moves the conversation forward and is deliberate. There is a structure to the interviews, and they are listening to the guest and responding intelligently.

A great host also has a sensitive ear and can adapt to the topic and guest as needed. Can the host match the energy and tone that you want? Or do they sound like they could be doing an interview for any show, on any station?

Another requisite skill for hosts is performance. Often, we like to think of broadcasters as serious journalists, and forget they are also performers. "The best host is a curious journalist, who knows how to peel back the layers of the story, but they're also great performers in the best sense of the word," Jay Kernis says, "That studio and that mic are their stage; they know how to claim it, grab your interest and hold it. They know your time is valuable and they honor that. They're the kid at the cool table and boy, you'd love to sit with them. This show allows you spend time with them."

Why is Terry Gross such an enduring and popular host? Because she can take a subject like the conservation of Purple Lilliput Mussels and make it interesting. How often have you heard a promo for *Fresh Air* and thought, "I don't want to hear that"? Then you heard a bit of the actual interview and found yourself unable to turn it off. A great host makes you care about unfamiliar issues and people who may seem uninteresting at first hearing.

I've used the word curious more than once, and want to explain what I mean by it. A great host is connected. Guests will often make references to TV shows and movies. They might say, "That guy reminds me of Frank Underwood." The host has to both recognize that the guest is referring to the show *House of Cards* and understand that the listener may not get the reference. So the host must ease in and say, "You mean, the ruthless politician played by Kevin Spacey on the show *House of Cards*?"

To do that, the host has to watch TV shows and movies, read comics and books, listen to music, and read gossip blogs; not because it's assigned, but because they have a curious mind and an insatiable intellectual appetite. All that information shouldn't result in a know-it-all attitude. Knowledge must be used in service of the audience, not to make listeners feel they've missed something.

Those are all the qualities you're seeking in a host. What should you avoid? Flashy personalities with whom you feel a bond and whom you like personally. If they're in it because they want lots of people to listen to them, they're probably not a great host. Not for public broadcasting, anyway. Direct them to commercial talk radio, post haste. Some hosts are bullies, but you can watch for that on the front end. Steer clear of people who've done old-school talk shows, in which they ruled. Those hosts developed at a time when they didn't have to adhere to more rigorous standards and they're often not amenable to change.

Stop hiring the people who have good voices and big personalities. It is absolutely crucial that you have someone who is a team player and a positive influence, who takes that as a serious part of their job. It needs to be a person who has done the work themselves, not someone who's always had assistants and producers, someone who has respect for their staff and doesn't expect more out of staff than they are willing to do. -- Alex Cohen, host of Take Two on KPCC

The role of host has inflated many an ego, so don't start with an ego that's already bloated and oppressive. A great host is gracious and lets the guest shine. Don't be lured by a reporter or commentator with a large personality. The truth is, a host has to tamp down his or her personality because the show is not about the host. A host is the conduit between the guest and the listener.

A really common problem in recruitment is some managers are afraid of hosts, or at least wary. So they may hire someone who seems easy to control. But great hosts are not compliant. "By definition, someone who's going to be good at that job is someone who can think for themselves," says NPR host Michel Martin, "That's why comedians are good guests and hosts and actors are not. You are looking for someone that you can work with, but not 'handle.' Ask yourself this: do you want to be successful or do you want to be comfortable? You don't want a fan girl or boy. A good host is skeptical and questions things, and a host that challenges the guests is also a host that's going to challenge the management." It doesn't make the manager's job any easier, but it does make the radio better.

The best hosts aren't universally liked, either. They can be polarizing. It's much scarier to hire a host who generates no emotional reaction than one who inspires a few complaints. As long as your host doesn't cross the line into editorializing or bullying guests (or staff), then the occasional complaint is a sign they are doing their jobs. A host who bullies people is a real concern, though. So, watch carefully for someone who crosses this line.

That said, one vital trait you're looking for is emotional stability. Every day, a host is under incredible pressure. Hosting a talk show is the most exposed a journalist will ever be. Hosts have to reveal something (but not too much!) of themselves. They have to make themselves vulnerable. When there's a factual error in the script, no listener thinks, "Boy, his producers really screwed up there." Instead, they think, "Geez, that guy never gets his facts straight." Hosts are juggling an incredible number of tasks and facts in their heads while they're live on the air, performing, and trying to make a connection with a guest.

If your host is too high strung, if she's easily thrown off by mistakes and changes, if he's emotionally volatile, it's a recipe for disaster. To a certain extent, you have to rely on the honesty of your candidate's references on this issue. But you should make sure to ask about this specifically. Can the host handle their own mistakes? On live radio especially, hosts are often corrected. Can they handle that with grace?

I'll explain later how you can test for emotional stability during the audition process. Obviously, an audition is an artificial environment. Anyone can remain controlled for a short period of time. That's why a longer test period, a week ideally, is a good idea and well worth the investment. Paying the money for a longer audition time is much better than the cost of firing that host and looking for a new one six months down the road when you realize you hired the wrong person.

Public broadcasters have long functioned under the principle that all on-air talent can be trained to become a host, but it simply isn't true. As Jeff Hansen, formerly of KUOW, says, "In the past, we picked people who sounded good and could read copy and could push buttons." That was common practice in public broadcasting for decades. Now, many people are making the same mistake in their podcasts. Time to evolve.

HOW TO TEST A POTENTIAL HOST

A good host must be comfortable in front of the mic. That sounds simple, but it's really not. They need to be comfortable talking with presidents and janitors, kindergarten teachers and CEOs, liberals and conservatives, gays and straight, people whose beliefs they share and those they shun. They should express their personality with confidence, and be fully themselves, without being so afraid of making a mistake that they don't listen and engage in productive conversation.

A strong host is also a good extemporaneous speaker. They can't just read scripts; they should be good storytellers. These are all things you can test in an audition.

Here are exercises to use to audition your potential host.

1. Present the host with five interview scripts. Two will be pre-recorded and three will be live. Make sure they write their own questions, based on basic facts about the guests you provide as well as their own prep. Each interview should be unique in scope (i.e., obit, breaking news, book interview)

2. Include some names that may be difficult to pronounce and some facts that might be sketchy, outdated, or suspect.

   WHAT YOU'RE LISTENING FOR: Does the host re-write the intros? Do they ask questions of the producers, verify pronunciations and facts? It's necessary that your host be self-motivated, with an instinctive need to do the job right. Be sure you have more talking points than you think you need.

3. Ask the hosts to write their own continuity. Provide audio clips and a template and have them write your billboard and promos.

   WHAT YOU'RE LISTENING FOR: Can they write for themselves in a characteristic, clear way that can be read without stumbling? Is it conversational? The writing should be crisp, clear, active, simple and concise. It should reflect the host's unique voice, with no flowery language and no drama, or worse, melodrama.

4. Pre-record two interviews

   WHAT YOU'RE LISTENING FOR: Do the pieces have shape? Is there a beginning, middle and end? How close did they get to the target time? Were the questions too long, or were they succinct and clear?

5. Record a live show, using the interviews you've prepared, just as you would do it in real time. However, disrupt the host. Have a guest not show up or have the guest's line drop. Interrupt with breaking news and run in with an AP story for the

host to handle as he or she can. Prep them for one interview and change it while they're doing it.

WHAT YOU'RE LISTENING FOR: How calm are they? Things will go wrong during real broadcasts. Is your host able to calmly continue on the air while handling a crisis? Does the host reveal her personality without talking too much about themselves or their opinions? Do you trust this person? Close your eyes and listen. Does this host put a spotlight on the guest or himself?

6. Have the host re-take a couple of things, like an intro or the billboard. Ask them to change tone or change words. You can experiment with giving them incorrect verbiage.

WHAT YOU'RE LISTENING FOR: How well do they take direction? Can they change their tone, or do they resist changing their writing? Your host should not only be willing to take direction, but actually able to carry out those instructions.

7. Separately from the one-hour show, record the host telling you an off-the-cuff anecdote, any interesting story they know, even the plotline of a movie. You can ask them to brag for a moment. It should take five minutes or less.

WHAT YOU'RE LISTENING FOR: Can they tell an anecdote? They might be nervous during the show itself, so this can reveal whether or not your candidate can talk like a human being and sound personable and articulate. If they sound stiff during the show recording, this exercise will tell you if they can be trained to sound more human or not. If they're stiff, formal or impersonal in both the show and this anecdote, they are probably not the right host.

8. Ask your candidate to listen to their own performance and critique it.

   WHAT YOU'RE LISTENING FOR: How honest are they? Can they spot significant mistakes or are they pointing out the most minor errors they can find? Can they tell the difference between something that needs fixing and something that was just a blunder?

9. Have your hiring committee listen closely to the interviews.

   WHAT YOU'RE LISTENING FOR: A great thing to hear from a host during a two-way is, "I don't know that! Guide me." Despite careful prep, guests will say surprising things (we hope). Can the host acknowledge they don't know everything and ask curious questions? The host should make other people feel comfortable. That personality trait, the ability to put others at ease in a conversation, cannot be trained. Listen for it now. And here's the big one: follow-up questions. Very rarely does someone give an answer that's sufficient. If a host doesn't have follow up questions, that's a big red flag. Don't tell them; see if they do it naturally. Your host should be relaxed, with energy, as if she's saying, "Welcome to this conversation with equals." They ask the questions you would ask. Do you hear warmth? Do they help you understand the issue just through their questions?

The truth is, a large number of people who host podcasts and radio shows do not have the natural ability for it. And that's not only true at local stations. There have been bad hires made at the networks as well. You can't throw someone on the air and hope they get better. In the end, you have to be honest when someone doesn't have what it takes. Perhaps they have no depth or maturity, no originality.

A mediocre host imitates the sound of NPR. He often sounds like he's reading copy, because he is. Maybe she needs to be told, word-for-word, what to say. When I asked my experts about the most common mistake hosts make, the number one answer was, "Read copy off the page." Your host should be able to read a weather forecast and sound like a likeable human being. It's conversation, not PowerPoint. That can't be taught. Most skills can be honed and improved. This usually cannot.

If you have found a likely candidate, with natural ability, give them a chance to grow into the job. For a new host, give them about six months to become comfortable. After nine months, you will know for sure if they're going to work or not. It's best to be honest about that and make a clean break, if necessary. That's why it's important to sign only a one-year contract with your host at first.

During that year, bring in guest hosts to take the chair on a regular basis. That will allow you to listen for new talent and identify possible replacements and subs.

Of course, I hope you don't end up having to replace your host. I think we can all agree it's better to be careful in the hiring than cautious in the firing. Take your time choosing a host. Find someone worth the investment who will be a positive force in your organization. And let me say it one more time, just for giggles: don't trust your gut.

WHAT DOES A HOST DO?

Should hosts write their own scripts? Edit interviews? Have management responsibilities? Yes, yes, yes, and also no. It all depends on workflow and the kind of work environment your host needs to in order to perform at their best.

That said, there are normal, standard duties for a host. Start with those and adapt as needed for the host you have. Just remember to meet your host where he is. That means creating a job description that best suits your host's capabilities and strengths, instead of writing a list of tasks and forcing the host to conform. Hosting is a performance art. Each host's needs and capabilities will be individual and unique. They're not delicate flowers (or shouldn't be), but each will have their own way of working.

Every host should write, and write a lot. No one should write better for the host than the host. A good host won't need to be told to do this. She'll want to rewrite intros and continuity to put them in her voice. She's the one saying it on the air; once those words come out of her mouth, they are hers. She should go over every word and make it her own. This requires a good amount of time. In a staff of five people, you will have four people writing content and one host going through it all. Assume this task will take several hours every day.

The script must serve the host. If producers write questions, they are merely suggestions. The host, in the end, decides where the segment will begin and where it will end and what it will cover. While the show is on the air, the host is the executive producer. He decides if an interview will go long and extend over a break, whether he wants to dump the next segment, and whether he'll break in with a news update. So the host has to make sure every script has what he needs in it and is formatted in a way he can follow.

To do that though, the host has to absorb the material well enough to write questions and ask follow-up questions. That means the host should be reading all of the prep that producers provide and, as much as possible, doing their own research as well. This will take up the bulk of their day. Producers should have the scripts done for the next day 24 hours in advance, so the host can spend each day prepping for tomorrow.

Preparation, or lack of it, is what distinguishes many hosts. When a story is pitched, the host should continue asking questions until he understands the core issue. The host should be able to express what they want in a segment so everyone understands. A vital part of the job is communicating with producers, making sure everyone is on the same page. Hosts should be able and willing to hear feedback from producers and, when needed, change course.

A host will also need to engage in community outreach. Your host is a voice of the station and the connection to her is emotional. Having your host meet listeners in person is great for the station's brand, but it also maintains a strong connection between the host and her audience. It's easy, when you are sitting in a sound-proofed studio every day, to start feeling isolated and lose your visceral bond with the people you are serving. Radio is an inherently intimate medium, but the intimacy should be mutual. Get your host out of the studio and into the real world when you can.

You should have realistic expectations about how many events and panels your host can attend, though. You hired them to host a show; don't let ancillary duties pull them from their primary responsibility. Burnout is a real danger, so make sure you don't load too many extra tasks on his calendar. Allow your host to focus on the main task: hosting.

STEP TWO: DEVELOP YOUR TALENT

Hosts need coaches. That may seem obvious, but most stations and networks don't coach their hosts. Many don't even do regular air checks. Just like opera singers, hosts will need coaching for the entirety of their careers, even after they've been in the business for decades.

This is about more than just catching mistakes. This is about remaining engaged with your host. We'll take a closer look at this in the section about managing shows. But it's important for managers to practice active listening and to respond both positively and negatively to the host and the staff. Do you have a tense relationship with your host? When was the last time you sat down and talked about her work, what you liked, what you thought could improve?

Distance doesn't lend enchantment in this relationship. Good hosts crave feedback. They don't want to stagnate; they want to know what's working and what isn't and why. They want to improve. If you aren't qualified to criticize, find a coach who can come by a few times a year. There are lots of qualified coaches out there.

A word of caution: don't hire a host who doesn't have the raw talent to hold down a show and hope you can fix that through training and development. "You can train to a certain point," says NPR's former programming chief Ellen McDonnell, "But after that point, it won't get any better. You can help them sound more relaxed, you can help them stop stumbling, but there's a certain percentage of performance and stage presence that can't be taught. They need to seem relaxed and human, but brilliant at the same time. That's either in them or it isn't."

NPR's Lynn Neary echoes that sentiment. "The hardest thing is to let yourself be yourself and I have no idea how to teach that," she says. "For some people it is a natural talent, a function of their charismatic personalities (think Susan Stamberg, Scott Simon). Some people grow into the role and some people never fully do." So as you plan how to develop your hosting talent, make sure you focus on those skills that can be trained and don't waste time on those that simply can't be learned.

The best training tool for a host is the air check. We'll talk through that process in a moment. The air check isn't a miracle cure and shouldn't be the only tool you use. Two other skills should be developed and trained: vocal presence and crafting interviews.

One of the hardest things to do when you're moving a reporter into a hosting role is to break down "Reporter Voice." Reporters often have a very matter-of-fact, formal tone. NPR's Rachel Martin calls it the "Sell-It Voice." It can be difficult for talent to relax and find their natural pacing and sound. This process can take months, if not longer. Rachel Martin had to make that difficult transition from reporter to host. So did I. It can be done, but it takes years of work.

Jeff Hansen, formerly of KUOW, says he has sometimes hired people because he liked how they sounded. Then, as soon as they got into the job, they fell into the typical pub radio voice. Listen to how your host talks normally. Does it match the way they sound on the air? If not, you need to sit down and do some exercises.

Go back to the audition exercise you used before you hired them. Have them sit in the studio and tell you a story and record it. "You just saw a car accident. Tell me what happened." The aim is to find out how the host sounds when they're not on the air, and record it. Then, sit with your host and play a sample of how they sound when they're relaxed and natural. Compare that with a sample of what they sound like when they're using their "Host Voice" or "NPR Voice." This is a good final check for you as well: if you can't hear the difference, you may not be the right person to air check your host.

The point is not to nitpick the pitch of the voice or the sound (forget vocal fry!). Your goal is to help your host know what it feels like and sounds like to be relaxed and natural so they can get into that mindset when they're going on the air. Hosts can get caught up with how they sound, but it's incredibly counterproductive to encourage them to obsess about it. Just tell them to tell their story as though they're in a bar. Then record them reading copy and play them both back. A radio script should be a horrible print piece. Just talk!

What is Vocal Fry?

Vocal fry is the gritty, gravelly, popping sound a voice makes when it's vibrating at the extreme low end of the person's range. You can create it now by imitating the sound of a creaking door. Vocal fry is not a modern phenomenon and it's not specific to females. Noam Chomsky's speech is littered with fry and some cultures use it as an inflection to distinguish between vowels. Vocal fry is not harmful to the voice unless it's overused. So, is vocal fry a good or bad thing? It's neither. It's just something you can use or not use. Just be careful not to overuse it, as it's possible it can harm your vocal cords.

From my years of singing opera, I can tell you the voice doesn't sound the same inside your head as it does when it leaves your mouth. It's simple acoustics. Get your host out of his head. Help him learn what he needs to do to relax. Does he need quiet or to chat before the show? What will get him to that point where he's speaking like a regular human being? That's what you want to find. Help him identify what that feels like, and then help him learn to replicate it.

You should also give your host a chance to practice interviewing. Make these sessions few and far between, because this is what they do every day. It's entirely understandable that they don't want to interview people all day and then sit down and do it more "just for practice".

There's real value in doing practice interviews from time to time, during which you can stop and start and try different things. This is also a great time to listen to examples of other hosts and analyze what other people are doing that works and what doesn't and why.

Do a bunch of short interviews with different people. Try using various formats. First, imagine you're trying to make news, so try to get the guest to say something newsworthy. Second, make the guest reveal something personal about themselves. Third, have a little fun. Do a "Desert Island Music" interview or something that allows your guest to talk about himself in a different way.

This will help you identify habits or quirks the host might have. Sometimes they creep in and no one notices. For example, a guy named Gustavo Almodovar was a reporter for WFTV in Florida some years back. He signed off in exactly the same way at the end of every report, and couldn't seem to do it without snapping his head to the left. His manager may not have noticed it, but it's impossible to ignore when you see the compilation video on YouTube. Almodovar's is a physical tic, but the principle holds for verbal habits as well: they creep in. A host can reflexively say "uh-huh" or "sure" until it becomes irritating to the listening ear.

Doing great interviews requires practice, and the best practice doesn't occur when the host is on the air and the stakes are high. Rehearsing on the air is a bad idea. Journalist Jamila Bey says when she was reporting, she noticed she was asking lazy questions. So she focused on just that, making sure she didn't ask any question that she would hesitate to air. This requires discipline and focus and practice. Radio station KUOW in Seattle actually offers an interview-intensive course to employees. It's a full week of workshops, eight hours a day. Interviewing is not casual conversation.

Improv is also an amazingly effective on-air training tool, and not just for your host. It teaches your staff how to think on their feet, how to listen carefully and how to react quickly. I can't say enough about the ways in which improv help your employees grow. There are multitudes of talented improv teachers out there, and pages and pages of guides to doing improv with your office, class, and friends. Check them out. Use them.

At least a third of the people I interviewed for this book mentioned improv as a valuable tool. And it makes sense. As Lynn Neary says, when your show is live, "you have to let go of the idea of perfection. It's live. Unexpected things will happen. You have to just improvise and move on." Since your host will have to improvise from time to time, it might be worthwhile to train them in how to do that.

Honestly, the kind of training you choose to use is less important than the fact that you're invested in development. If you don't schedule training opportunities, it's all too easy to let a year go by without holding any workshops. I'd suggest putting reminders into your calendar.

THE AIR CHECK

Please air check me. - Celeste Headlee, host (to her managers)

Ideally, you should air check the host every week. But if you can only do it once a month, that's still great. Heck, if the host only gets an air check once every six months, that's still better than what usually happens, which is nothing. Most stations don't give their hosts regular air checks, which is nuts! The single most important thing you do is create an on-air product. Why would you attend endless meetings on marketing strategies and fundraising and invest absolutely no time in improving your core competency?

I guarantee your audience is air checking your host every day. In 2014, *The Daily Beast* published a piece called "Shows on NPR, Ranked in Order from Glorious to Unbearable." Take a look at it. Yes, the author doesn't really understand which shows are produced by NPR and which aren't, but she's pretty incisive in her criticism and praise. She's listening critically, as are many listeners. In the comments on a Howard Stern interview, someone said, "Have you ever noticed that Stern has all the answers before he even knows the question? He inserts his own answers and has to be corrected time after time." That's spot on, and Howard should hear it from his executive producer, not a random listener.

There should be regular conversations between talent and management, and 80 percent of the comments should be supportive: "I liked that, do more of that. How can I help you do that more?" On occasion, a correction will be in order.

Do you like sitting down in a meeting so someone can pick apart everything you've done? Neither do I. It's a safe bet your host doesn't either, and it's important you establish a positive, constructive atmosphere in the air check. You don't want the host to dread it. That's not the best way to achieve your goal, which is to help your host grow and improve. Don't listen to an hour of radio and let 50 minutes of great stuff pass in one ear and out the other while you note down 10 minutes of errors. .

Hosts need feedback, but it can't be editorial. It's not appropriate for administrations to criticize the choice of guests or stories *to the host*. I'll explain later how to establish a process for editorial complaints, but the air check is not the right place for that. And you absolutely can't give feedback while the show is on the air. Let me repeat that, so I know for sure that you got it: Do not give feedback while the show is on the air, not even to the producers in the control room! No quick emails dashed off while you're listening at your desk. No bursting into the control room to ask, "What the hell was that music?"

Bide your time and wait until they're off the air. I'm going to say this again later, to be triply sure that you've got it, because I know how tempting it is to address issues immediately. It's hard for me, too! When I'm hosting and something goes wrong, I want to rush into the control room during the next break and ask what the heck happened.

But both the host and the staff are in a heightened emotional state when the show is live. They're tense and stressed and criticism will hit them especially hard. Ask yourself what the point is of critiquing something. If you're angry and trying to punish your employees, then burst into the control room and start criticizing. If your purpose is to find out what went wrong and make sure it doesn't happen again, then wait until your comments can be heard and addressed calmly, rationally and productively.

Meanwhile, back at the air check... In your session, play examples of something that worked well. "Listen to what you did there," you can say. "That's great. How can we do more of that?" Pick one thing for the host to work on and master. Remember Jamila Bey and her effort to stop asking lazy questions? She chose a simple, very specific goal and practiced until she mastered it. It's often best to start small, as you do when you're paying off credit card debt. Pay off the smallest balance first, and then move on to the next one.

The bottom line? Someone has to be paying attention, so problems can be addressed promptly and early. You can't kick the can down the road. That establishes bad precedent and tradition. Set a regular schedule for air checks and then stick to it.

THE TWO-WAY (HOW TO DO A GREAT INTERVIEW)

This is arguably the most important section of this entire guide. Interviewing isn't easy. It's both a science and an art. It requires skill, craft, and a touch of magic. Anyone who works in broadcasting has room to improve their interviewing skills, no matter how long they've been in the profession. When I'm listening to podcasts and shows, the most common complaint I have is that the interviews are terrible, and no one ever trained the host in how to interview well.

Hosting is about interviewing. That's the core job. Even for reporters, a good story begins with good interviews. The difference is, reporters can be a little lazy in their interviews. They can ask questions in any order for as long as the interviewee will talk. A host has to have the shape of the conversation mapped out in advance, in her head. She has to know the beginning and the end and what it takes to get there.

For some reason, we rarely train broadcasters in how to interview well. We hold workshops in writing, in social media, in finding sources, while we rarely teach people how to ask questions and how to structure conversations. This is not just important for hosts! Reporters waste untold hours looking for a good 20-second bite, when being more efficient from the start of the interview could cut that raw audio from 35 minutes down to five or ten.

There is no skill in broadcasting more basic than effective questioning. Even producers need to learn it to improve their pre-interviews. And here's the good news: while hosting requires some innate ability, interviewing can be learned and improved through training.

First, the basics. Most interviews are one of two types: the informational, and the profile. In the first, you're eliciting information or expert analysis on a topic. This includes MOS (man-on-the-street) interviews, such as talking to a homeowner who lost her house to a tornado or a kid who's been bullied. It also includes conversations with legal scholars about the Supreme Court or a NASA scientist talking about Mars or a pundit discussing the latest immigration bill.

The second kind of interview is generally called a profile: chatting with an author about their new book or musician about their new album, or any person you're talking to simply because they're interesting, important, or have a surprising story to tell. This can also include people who've been instrumental in a headline event, like Captain "Sully" Sullenberger, who landed his US Airways plane on the Hudson River in 2009.

Obviously, there are many other variations on the simple interview. There are panel discussions and interviews with politicians that are neither a profile nor particularly informational. It doesn't matter what kind of interview you're doing or how many guests you have at the table, your technique doesn't change one iota. The purpose of any interview, no matter whom the subject, is to showcase your guest's unique knowledge and experience. I'll be even more explicit: the focus of any interview is the interviewee.

I break up my approach to doing two-ways into nine parts, and I strongly suggest you choose one at a time and master it before moving on to another. Here are the basic steps to a great interview:

1. Read the Book
2. Choose Your Focus
3. Create a Structure
4. Ask Good Questions
5. Get the Best Out of the Guest
6. Handle Difficult Guests
7. Practice Active Listening
8. Manage the Clock
9. Wrap It Up

These are more or less in chronological order, walking you through from the moment an interview is assigned, all the way until you say goodbye and thank you to your guest.

READ THE BOOK (PREP)

> *Wow, you really read the book. - John Irving,*
> *after I interviewed him*

Step one: read the book. This may sound overly simplistic, but sadly, no. I'm daily shocked by the number of reporters and anchors who don't know the material their guest is there to talk about. They don't read the book, watch the speeches, study the op-eds, listen to the music, see the show, or glance over the study before they talk to the interviewee about their conclusions.

Let me give you a particularly egregious example of this: the *Morning Joe* interview of Russell Brand in 2013. Brand is there to talk about the tour of his new show, "Messiah Complex." Mika Brzezinski introduces Brand by saying her colleague might undress for the comedian's benefit. They then spend a minute talking about his appearance and his boots. 90 seconds in, we finally get a question and it is, "Messiah Complex. Do you have one?" The interview goes completely off the rails after that.

At one point, Brzezinski says, "That sounds dead serious," as though she's surprised. Perhaps she saw "comedian" on the rundown next to Brand's name and that's as far as her preparation went. I could spend half an hour explaining all the mistakes made in that travesty of a segment, but I'll restrict myself to the glaring lack of preparation.

You don't sit down with Russell Brand without at least knowing that he's a standup comedian, but I would recommend you make sure to watch a few clips of his material, read the summary of his newest project and read a few of the outstanding pieces he's written for The Guardian. His writing on Margaret Thatcher and his piece on the criminalization of drug addiction are brilliant: articulate, smart and "dead serious." Reading just the first few paragraphs of those pieces is enough to tell you that Brand is a thinker. More importantly, you could watch the piece he's there to talk about, "Messiah Complex." It's funny, yes, but it's also intellectually complex and nuanced. I would never begin an interview with this man by talking about his chest hair and his silver boots.

If you think the "Morning Joe" incident was rare, I refer you to any author who's done broadcast interviews while on a book tour. I had the great pleasure of talking to John Irving about his novel "Last Night in Twisted River." When we finished, Mr. Irving shook my hand warmly and said, "You really read the book." I was shocked! Who goes into an interview with John Irving and doesn't read his book? But he's hardly the only author to say something like that to me. I had always assumed that if you were going to question someone of his stature, you would do your homework. Turns out, that's not the case in general. Salman Rushdie told me once, "It's always such a pleasure to talk to someone who's read my book. It's so rare."

The predictable pushback here is hosts are on tight deadlines and sometimes don't get these assignments until the day before the interview. As a host who worked for years on a four-hour, live daily news program called "The Takeaway", I understand this as well as anyone can. It's quite true that prepping for an interview sometimes means working through your family dinner or opting not to go to the movies with your spouse. In the long-term, that's a personal choice you have to make about the kind of life you'd like to lead and how to find a healthy career/life balance. In the short term, that's the job and you have to get it done.

If you really don't have time, you should be completely above board about your lack of preparation. I've done this many times. "I apologize, I didn't have time to finish your book, so I'm coming to this conversation much like our listeners are. Why did you decide to write on this topic?" I've used some version of that question on numerous occasions.

Preparation should be careful and deliberate for all interviews, though, not just with authors. Listen to the work of *Morning Edition* host Steve Inskeep. He comes in armed with so much information, he's prepared to push back on his guests or follow whatever thread emerges. In an interview, you have to think like a debater as you prepare and then become a neutral party on the air. You should understand your guest's case as well as your own. Your preparation has to be good enough to enable you to follow your guest wherever he goes, or to recognize when he's wandered off topic.

As NPR host Michel Martin says, "Research is not about the results on the first page of your Google search." Try to take the long view, see if the guest's perspective has changed over time. Compare what they said in 2009 with what they say now.

If you read other interviews, you'll discover most prominent people get asked the same questions over and over. Be prepared to *not* ask those questions of your guest. You don't need to duplicate someone else's work, especially in this age when any of your listeners can immediately access most of those other interviews on their smartphones.

Be as prepared as possible, without pretending to be an expert. As the saying goes, "You don't have to be dead to write an obituary." Your guest has been booked because she's the expert. Let her tell us the facts. Just make sure you've read the book, watched the movie or read the study.

If you know a guest may be boring, dry, or a bad talker, you might be tempted to forego the preparation. Perhaps you think you won't need a lot of in-depth information because the guest won't open up or go deep. The fact is, you'll need *more* information if the guest isn't strong. You'll have to fill in gaps in the conversation, tell parts of the story. Here's the bottom line: the worse the interview, the more your preparation matters.

Even when interviewing someone as familiar as Gregg Allman, I go back and listen to his music. I've never finished an interview and thought, "Boy, I really did too much preparation for that."

CHOOSE YOUR FOCUS

Once your preparation is done, you must decide what the interview is about. What are the essential questions you need to have answered?

Even if the purpose of your interview is purely informational, as in talking with a BBC reporter on the streets of Cairo on the day after a military coup, you have to choose a focus. There are too many directions it could go, and too much information to cover. In the situation I just mentioned, you probably want to get the most current update, but you may want to ask a question that hasn't been addressed in other coverage, like "Who is leading the military forces?"

Other interviews are not so straightforward. If you're interviewing a legal expert about the Trayvon Martin case or a foreign policy expert on Syria, there are quite literally dozens of questions you could ask and you won't have time for all of them. One way or the other, you have to narrow down the conversation and make sure you've gotten the best possible material from your guest, for your audience.

Here is an easy rule of thumb: ask about what only your guest can tell you. Let me explain further. Raw data, dates, numbers and other facts can be relayed in a 40-second spot. There is a reason you're doing an interview instead of a news update: what is it? What can that person tell you that is different from what any other guest might say? Does your legal expert specialize in medical evidence? Has he or she argued a case in which the decision to charge the defendant with murder instead of manslaughter became crucial to conviction? You can only answer these questions if you've done your homework.

Research is becoming a running theme in this guide.

If you can't find a specific focus, it means you probably need to go back a step and do more preparation. Find out what your guest specializes in and ask about that. Everyone is an expert in something, even the 14-year-old high school freshman and the 85-year-old retired veterinarian. I'm always shocked when hosts interview musicians and don't ask about the music. Instead, they ask about their mother, childhood sex abuse, politics or any number of totally unrelated things. Maybe those issues are important, but if you're talking to Melissa Etheridge, talk to her about music! Music is the reason she's famous. Music is what she loves and it's what she's an expert in. Focus on that, and let the other stuff come up naturally.

The focus can also be described as "the reason you're doing this interview." For example, some people were angry with NPR's Michel Martin for doing an interview with David Duke, the former Grand Wizard of the Ku Klux Klan. But she wanted to let listeners who would normally ignore

Duke completely, hear his point of view. She was absolutely clear about her agenda and never lost her focus. An interview can't succeed unless you decide why you're having it.

CREATE A STRUCTURE

Once you have a focus, you can create a structure. Every interview has a beginning, a middle and an end. This is what really separates a host interview from one conducted by a reporter. A host's questions are heard on the air and she creates the arc of the story through her questions. You can't cut it up and write a story around selected clips. Hosts help connect the dots. They tell a story over time.

Sometimes you have to adjust the starting point to make sure you reach the ending you want. Do you know what your final question is? You should, because if you don't, it will be impossible to decide what the middle should be about. The middle is the transition; it follows logically after the beginning and leads inevitably to the end. Think I'm being condescending? I'm not. Take a listen to some radio pieces and you'll hear many that are simply a collection of unconnected questions.

What is the shape of the interview? What are the key points? This can be laid out in a few brief notes on the script, but you need to know the structure before you begin. What do you want to spend two minutes on? What needs four minutes?

When you have multiple guests, it's usually best to start with a "real person", if you have one, so there's human interest value. It also helps you establish immediately why we should care about this topic. A woman with a learning disabled kid explains how her child was isolated from his peers at school and given less attention or resources. Then your academic comes in to give context, explain if this is common or not. Your expert adds depth of knowledge and perspective, but your regular person is the one your listener will likely relate to.

The arc is there as a constant reminder about why anyone cares. You can do minutiae for one or two questions and then get back to reality: why do all those details matter? What do these numbers mean? Why should you care?

Draw your listeners in with your short, sharp intro, and then begin with the tension in the story. In our example of the kids with special needs, the tension is the child who's been neglected. That's where you start. In a story about polluted water, the tension might be a person who's become ill. Move on from the tension to one question you really need to get answered, then you can continue with that thread or move on to something else, based on what your guests have said. The arc of the conversation is the foundation on which your conversation is built.

Over the course of an interview, a host may have to edit and alter the arc many times: and she has to do it in her head. As the poet Robert Burns said, even the best laid plans "o' mice an' men gang aft a-gley." If you start with a well-defined arc though, it's much easier to amend it than it is to build a structure on the fly to salvage an interview that's gone far into left field and seems destined to keep wandering.

Do you know a host who consistently records 30-40 minute conversations that have to be edited down to 8 minutes? While there are many possible explanations for this, one of the most common is the host isn't arcing the conversation.

The host is not keeping to the rigorous discipline of editing on-the-fly. Not every interview I do comes in to time, but I try to make that happen every time because I think it makes for stronger journalistic pieces, not to mention saving you hours of time cutting and pasting.

Just remember: a beginning, a middle and an end. Tell a story.

GOOD QUESTIONS

If the arc of the conversation is the trip from the lobby to the penthouse, your questions are the vehicle that carries you there. The quality of questions separates a good host from a great one.

As a rule of thumb, I follow the advice of legendary coach David Candow: stick with the five W's (who, what, where, when, why) and how. David said if you put a complicated question in, you'll get a simple answer coming out and vice versa. I've found this to be generally true. If you ask, "Did you feel scared?", the person will respond to the idea of "scared" instead of telling you how he felt. If you say, "The House recently passed its 5th overturn of the Affordable Care Act. Should health care advocates be worried?", then your guest will respond to "worried" instead of telling you what that means for advocates of universal health care.

The common pitfall here is to construct a question to demonstrate your knowledge or experience of a subject by including dates, data, numbers, and names. Some anchors like to mention their own history in covering a region or topic. To this, I say, "It's not about you." Neil DeGrasse Tyson doesn't care how much you know about astrophysics and Steven Spielberg couldn't care less that you dabbled in film direction as a student. Keep the focus on the guest always and in everything. That applies even when you interview another journalist about breaking news. As much as you can, let the reporter report.

A good discipline in solutions-based journalism is to practice the Three Whys -- a technique originally developed by Sakichi Toyota for the automaker. The principle behind this technique is that many problems have more than one root cause, and it may take a series of questions to get to the bottom of what happened.

It's quite simple in principle, but more difficult in implementation. You go for the why more than once, but without sounding like you're pestering.

Example:
1. Why have state test scores dropped by 17% this year? Answer: The teachers only had a couple weeks to prepare their classes.
2. Why? Answer: The federal NCLB testing was scheduled right before the state test.
3. Why? Answer: We didn't have any other good dates. There's too much testing in schools.

The Three Whys is one of the most efficient problem-solving techniques in business and it's an objective way for journalists to delve deeply into political, financial or social issues.

Here are more specific guidelines to asking good questions.

1. Ask one question at a time. Avoid this: "When did you first start playing soccer and why choose that sport instead of hockey, the sport that your dad

played?" When you ask multiple questions, the guest can choose what to answer. Also, you can stress them by forcing them to remember all that you asked. You're there to make things easy for your guest, and to let them speak.

2. <u>Avoid making statements instead of asking questions.</u> This one is debatable and as respected a source as NPR's Jonathan Kern, who created the network's training program, recommends using statements on a regular basis. I disagree with him on this. While I sometimes use statements to get a response from guests, I think they should be few and far between. Many's the time I've made a statement, only to see the guest looking at me blankly, waiting to respond to a question. But I refer you to Kern's book, *Sound Reporting,* for advice on how to use a well-constructed statement to have a natural conversation. One further note: a statement with an upward inflection at the end is not a question. And adding, "Could you talk about that?" doesn't turn your statement into a question, either.

3. <u>Don't ask a question you know the answer to.</u> Your producers will try to make you do this. "Actually ask a real question," NPR's Steve Inskeep says. "Having asked it, stop. Very often people will ask a question they imagine they already know the answer to, and they ask it in a way that shows they already know the answer. There's no suspense there. It sounds like the host is in on it with the guest. The host will say, 'Tell us about the time you went to Georgia and were arrested.' Instead, say, 'Tell us what happened when you went to Georgia.'"

4. <u>Don't say "some people"</u>. Ask for yourself.

5. <u>Don't ask multiple choice questions.</u> This is common. A host will say, "Were you scared? Calm? Or did you not even notice it was happening?" Instead, just ask them what it was like. You should jump in only if they're struggling to answer.

We learn more easily from stories than from statistics and details, so steer your guest away from reciting facts and figures. The interview should sound like you're saying, "Hello, friend in my home, let me introduce you to this other friend. Let me tell you why they're here and put them in context so you have a sense of who they are and why you should listen."

It's good to take your guest back to a formative moment and ask what they were thinking or feeling at the time. You can also ask what they saw and heard. That will help put them in the moment. What does the guest know now that would have been good to know at the time? And you can also research whatever it is they're working on, find out what's not working, and ask them why.

If the guest doesn't answer your question, you can say, "What I really wanted to know was…". Keep control of the interview at all times. Sometimes your guest will get off on a tangent. You should interrupt them. Kojo Nnamdi at WAMU in DC will finish his guest's thought and then bring him back to the point. He'll say, "And I know you've been complaining to the FCC about that, but let's get back to what happened during the broadcast."

If your question is short, sharp, and respectful, the audience will often be relieved you interrupted, instead of thinking you're rude. We'll talk more later about how to cut off a guest at the end of your interview. That's a different challenge.

One more tip: it's generally best to end the interview with a question that looks to the future. What happens next? What's your next project? Anything that gets the guest to talk about the story as ongoing is a good finish.

In addition to asking questions, you'll have to jump in from time to time for other reasons. For example, you should acknowledge when a guest mentions a fact you can't verify, like mentioning that Georgia has more unwed mothers than any other state. You can ask the guest what their source is, where the data come from.

You'll also have to jump in to provide what Jonathan Kern calls "drop-in context". That means you have to recognize terms and references guests use that listeners may not understand immediately. Do they say someone is "like Carrie Bradshaw"? You need to quickly explain she was Sarah Jessica Parker's character in *Sex in the City*. Do they mention ACORN? You should say that it stands for Association of Community Organizations for Reform Now and give enough context so listeners remember it was the voter registration group that was brought down by a hidden camera scandal.

You are at the helm of this ship: keep relaxed control at all times. Set up the topic clearly and bring the audience along with you every step of the way. Keep the conversation moving among the guests, even the bad talkers. If you have three people at the table and you ignore one of them, the audience will notice and they'll think you're being rude. Own your chair. You have to believe you belong there, although that doesn't mean you should ever pretend to know more than you do. Be honest about what you know and what you don't. You can't be any smarter than you are.

Sometimes, you will have to stop someone who's talking too long. If you don't, listeners might think, "Why is this person droning on?" Interrupt them by saying something like, "I think what you're saying is....." or "Let me bring this other guest in here...". The person you're most concerned with is the audience, not the guest. People don't like hearing someone being rude, but they also want the conversation to have forward momentum at all times.

Also, do not allow one guest to attack another. Say something like, "We're not having that here" or "I'm going to stop you there." Take control. Have courage. Be firm.

You're storytelling as a host and constructing a piece just as a reporter does with actualities. The difference is, you're doing it live. You're the narrator. If someone says something that doesn't make sense, you have to jump in and make sense of it. You weave the through line. What's the next question that arises naturally? Let's answer that or go to another guest.

If an interview is boring, that's often because there's no suspense or tension. What's at stake? Something important should always be at stake. It doesn't have to be life or death. Steve Inskeep tells a story about an interview he heard when he was in Morehead, Kentucky. The anchor brought on a guy who was in charge of encouraging tourism in Morehead. The anchor's first question was, "Who the heck would want to come here?"

Leading the segment off with that question grabbed Steve's attention, and probably the attention of other listeners as well. Asking a direct, simple surprising question can turn a boring interview like that into an entertaining segment.

Practice asking great questions. Hosting is all about interviews, and interviews are all about questions.

GET THE BEST OUT OF THE GUEST

Any interview is only as good as your guest. The reality is, you will have to interview a lot of mediocre talkers. Still, there are ways to get the best out of any guest, articulate or not.

Most guests will be at least a little uncomfortable. You do this every day; they don't. Give them an attractive place to wait, greet them warmly and chat them up. Not too much! You don't want them spilling everything you want them to say in the interview. But you can give them coffee or water, tell them what else is happening in the show, set them at ease.

Picture your favorite doctor for a moment. What do you like about them? Often, they tell you what's going to happen, whether it will hurt, how long it will take to get test results. They tell you what's expected of you. They're clear and they keep you informed. You should give your guests the same information. Be totally clear about what's happening, what they'll hear, how long their segment will last, and that it won't hurt.

If it's live, show them the signal you give when you're running out of time. Tell them to forget the microphones, look at you and just talk. I often say, "I have so many questions. I'm really curious about this subject. I'm so glad

I have you here to talk about it." You should also spend a minute explaining what type of show it is. Their entire experience with public radio might be *All Things Considered*, so they've come in ready to be a bit more formal and brief. If they're thinking of *Fresh Air*, they might talk longer than you want and share long, detailed personal stories.

Also, regardless of how often this information was checked in pre-production, check the guests' personal details one more time by saying their name and title out loud and asking them to confirm that you have it right. It's much better that they correct you during the break than while you're on the air.

You can waste valuable air time if you ask your guest to relay information, simple dates and numbers. You can do that in copy, probably more efficiently and clearly. Get the information out of the way in the intro and begin the conversation at a place that really highlights your guest's expertise, or gets to the crux of the issue. I've heard countless interviews that should have actually started two minutes in, when they got to the good stuff. Forget the windup. Go straight to the pitch.

If you and your staff prepare carefully and do a pre-interview (an essential step that's too often bypassed), you can identify early any topics that are potentially problematic. These might include particularly emotional subjects (including those that get guests angry) or topics that elicit an overly technical response, something we call "going into the weeds". Handle these subjects early and save yourself some time editing.

The pre-interview is your most powerful tool in dealing with emotional subject matter. We'll talk about this in more detail later, but if your producer has done the prep right, you'll know in advance what questions might make your guest break down. You probably want to avoid those; crying may be dramatic, but you're not hosting a Barbara Walters special. Listening to someone sob on the radio is usually painful and awkward, not powerful. The audience naturally wants to console the person who's crying, and you can't help but come across as the person who's asking questions while this person is falling apart. Either that or you have to stop the interview and console your guest, and then the segment has really gone off the rails. Welcome to the weeds.

Have some safe questions ready to direct the guest away from the area of sensitivity. If a guest begins to cry while talking about her deceased brother, spend a moment relaying information (i.e., "After the accident, dozens of people reached out to help you. I'm told that several neighbors even started a fundraising campaign to help cover the funeral expenses"), then you ask a question that leads them away from the sensitive area: "What kind of help did you get from friends and family?" If they are really beside themselves (this rarely happens), then you take over telling the story yourself based on your pre-interview notes. As you continue talking, they will have time to get themselves back under control.

Don't fear of silence after you ask a question. Your guest will often rush in to fill it, which is good. Keep your focus on your guests as much as possible. Your producers may message you or speak in your ear. That's normal for you, but it's disconcerting for the guest to see you turn away and start typing on your computer, or signaling to the control room.

Just remember to give your guest your full attention, ask strong questions, and then step out of the way to let your expert reveal his or her expertise. If it's breaking news and you're talking to a reporter who's done several interviews already, acknowledge that. You can say, "I know you've told this story a number of times, but walk me through it. Is there anything else you haven't had a chance to talk about? Help me advance the story."

Just like the rest of us, guests enjoy feedback. If something's interesting, say so! If it's surprising, say, "That's really surprising." It's not that hard to draw someone out and make them shine on air, if you can focus on them and not yourself or your staff. If they're funny, laugh.

HANDLE DIFFICULT GUESTS

Some interviews are trickier than others. It can vary with the type of guest you've booked. Perhaps the most difficult interviews are with politicians or advocates (especially biased pundits) who take a particular side on an issue, generally a political issue. I'm talking about the abortion rights advocate, the gay rights defender, the conservative Evangelical, the passionate environmentalist. Any time you are chatting with someone who has "talking points," you need to have your facts cold.

Many producers solve this issue by booking guests from both sides of an issue. Personally, I think this strategy has caused serious problems for our industry. In order to create a situation in which the journalist doesn't have to push back, we've constructed a false reality of "two sides to every story," in which all coverage of political issues is some version of "Crossfire." This has also led to the false equivalency that so many have rightly criticized the media for promoting.

If you are doing a story on the origin of the universe, you can't equate an astrophysicist with a local pastor whose opposition is based on faith. In that situation, you separate the two of them and make it clear that one point of view is based on scientific fact, the other on belief. That doesn't mean you show any less respect to the pastor, quite the contrary. But the two are apples and oranges and shouldn't be made to appear comparable. So, that's the first rule of thumb - don't wuss out and try to find a guest to do the push-back you don't want to do.

In a blog entry called "Journalists have to decide what to do about candidates who are climate change deniers," media critic Jay Rosen suggests a reporter should confront climate change deniers directly and openly. He suggests saying something like this: "The Intergovernmental Panel on Climate Change said in 1990, 'Emissions resulting from human activities are substantially increasing the atmospheric concentrations of greenhouse gases,' leading to global warming. They said it again in 1995. They said it again, but more strongly in 2001. They were even more emphatic in 2007. And in 2014 they said they were 95 percent certain that human action was the primary cause of global warming. The World Bank has come to similar conclusions. The position you have taken on this seems to suggest that you have better evidence than they do. Will you be making that evidence public? And may we have the names of your science advisors so we can ask them where they are getting their information?" This may seem controversial to some who are accustomed to the polite, courteous tone of most public radio hosts. However, if you don't challenge a guest when they say something untrue or questionable, you can leave the impression that what they're saying is established fact.

There are generally two reasons producers and hosts book guests to present opposing points of view. One is in the interest of balance, as I just described. Journalists worry if they contradict or argue with a guest, they'll be seen as taking a side or being partisan. The other reason is that pushback can be tough.

If you're going to point out flaws in a person's argument, you have to be informed enough to catch them. Often, the second guest is booked as an expert in the field. These are both perfectly valid reasons to get that second voice. I've made that choice many times. But don't be afraid make another choice.

Not every issue requires you to interview two people in opposition to each other. Often it's best to keep those voices separate. Don't try to book an argument. Hearing people argue rarely helps your listeners understand an issue. On the contrary, it's the worst possible method of relaying information.

As I said, you should treat the studio like your home, and all of the interviewees as invited guests. Neal Conan, former host of NPR's *Talk of the Nation,* spoke on this during a presentation in 2002: "If you invite a guest into your living room, you don't abide your other guests being rude to them. That is not the same as saying we cannot have vigorous discussions. We need to have vigorous discussions. But there is a difference between saying, 'Your idea is stupid,' and '*You* are stupid.' Big difference. All of us have to be careful about invective and screaming." Our goal is information, not confrontation.

If you decide to sit down with only one guest, then *do your homework*. Politicians, especially, will try to roll right over you. These interviews require the most prep work of any you'll do. Read what the person has written on the issues, listen to other interviews, do a pre-interview and make sure you are reasonably prepared for what they may say. Then, don't hide behind phrases like "Many people say...". Own your questions.

It is almost inevitable they will say something that's not entirely accurate or about which there are two defensible views. If they do, stop them. Don't allow politicians to continue talking after they've said something untrue or arguable, and don't be afraid to interrupt. Where accuracy is concerned, your responsibility is to the listener, not the guest.

Make them accountable for the claims they make. Be prepared to push back with facts, not opinions, so you can avoid an argument. If they say something that's incorrect, respond with, "That's an amazing statistic. Where are you getting that number?" Ask them, "What do you mean by that"? If they use a phrase like "outside agitators" or "extremists", make them be specific on what they mean. You should also ask for citations to back up their statements. If Ben Carson says the ACA is worse for blacks than slavery, Jamila Bey suggests you respond with, "That's a harsh contention. I'll have to ask for some facts. Where did that claim come from? Who's saying that? What is it based on?'" It's perfectly okay to ask them if what they've said is fact or opinion, and if they have data to back it up.

That's how you maintain your journalistic integrity while gently countering a guest. If they cite a poll, you cite an opposing poll (trust me, there will almost always be an opposing poll). Be polite, be respectful, but most of all, be right. Have your facts straight.

Politicians are human, too, remember. Connect with their humanity so you can steer them away from talking points. The only time politicians are valuable bookings is when you get them to respond to your questions truthfully, candidly, and briefly.

If your guest is nervous, here are tips on how to put them at ease. Talk to the guest before you begin, even if you only have a minute or two. This is usually done by producers, but not always. First, thank them for their time. Tell them what you plan to focus on. Let them know they don't need to give all their information in their first answer, and that the audience will retain information better if they give a bunch of short answers, as opposed to just a few long ones. Just chat with them for a moment. Talk to them about their family, their pets, sports, anything other than the topic you're about to interview them on. I tell them, "This is just you and me talking. I'm really fascinated by this and I have a lot of questions, so just talk to me."

Another difficult interview is the one with a scientist. In most cases, if you just let a scientist talk, your audience won't understand much of what's said and the interview will be a waste of time. As with most things, the best strategy is careful preparation. You should know the subject matter well enough to sum it up in plain language. Don't be afraid to get something wrong. That allows the guest to say, "That's not exactly what I meant." It's important you understand everything the scientist says. Don't assume that, even if you don't get it, the listener probably does. You *are* the listener. In the booking conversation and the pre-interview, listen closely to how they explain things. Don't book someone who can't talk.

You can prepare your scientist by telling them, "Imagine you're talking to your relatives, not your colleagues. You're at a family reunion, not the faculty lounge. How would you explain it to your grandma?" Tell them to stay away from acronyms and scientific terms, but be prepared to explain the acronym if they use one ("MRSA - you mean the antibiotic resistant staph infection?") or ask them, "What is MRSA?" No one expects you to have a degree in everything, so don't pretend you know more than you do. The host is the surrogate for the audience. Don't be afraid to say you don't understand.

Finally, there's another category of guest that can be difficult to handle and that's the passionate amateur. This includes your anti-vaxxer, anti-climate change advocate or anti-GMO activist. Amateur literally means one who loves and, of course, that love gives them one hell of a bias. This person is passionate about a scientific or medical issue, but has no scientific or medical training. First of all, be judicious in your booking. If you think the person's standpoint is completely wrong, don't book them.

You should never bring someone on the air just to tear apart their opinions. Remember, the studio is your home and they are invited guests. Don't engage a controversy just because it's controversial. That's not a constructive discussion. There's also an ethical issue here. If you're giving voice and airtime to an extremist position, you might be worsening an already dangerous situation.

If your guest expresses a questionable opinion, interject with "in your opinion." Listen with respect, remain calm, and don't get emotional. The best course is to include the science in the question and therefore, make the science a given. You don't want to get into a debate about established science. Say to them, "There is a medical consensus. Do you feel you're going against the grain? Can you see how other parents might feel that you're jeopardizing their kids' health?"

You can also politely bring up the basis for their claimed authority. For example, if you are interviewing Jenny McCarthy on vaccinations, you can ask her where she studied medicine, what studies she's relying on and who funded those studies. You can say, "Before we go on, because I very much want to hear your point of view, you are not a doctor, your background is in modeling and acting. What's the basis for your viewpoint?"

Again, the goal is not to tear apart the guest's opinion. If you've booked the guest in order to hear their view, then let them express themselves. Don't treat them like a scientific or medical expert. Just get their opinion and the basis for that opinion, then thank them and move on.

PRACTICE ACTIVE LISTENING

The most important skill for a host is active listening: engaged, curious, courteous, unwavering, and active listening. You can decide where an interview will begin and where you'd like it to end, but once you've started, the shape of the interview is entirely dependent on your guest and his responses.

Some hosts like to have a list of questions ready. Your script should include whatever you need to feel prepared and confident, but you will rarely use all the questions you've prepared in advance. I often only write two or three questions and then keep a list of pertinent facts nearby to consult.

If you're doing it right, the interview will not go entirely as planned and the guests will at some point say something surprising or unexpected. Then, you set your prepared questions aside and follow the new train of thought. Following a tangent can be a really compelling thing. There's nothing more ridiculous for listeners than to hear a guest say, "The book ended up being very personal because of my own history of abuse," followed by a host who asks about the publishing business or e-readers or why the main character is obsessed with Lindsay Lohan. You might as well start flashing a neon sign that says, "I'm not really listening to you." Stop looking ahead to your next question, stop worrying about what comes next, and really listen to what you're hearing.

One tactic is to put into your own words something the guest just said. You can say, "Let me be sure I understand you. I think what you're telling me is...." The guest may correct you, which is perfectly fine, but you have effectively signaled to the guest that you are listening and that you care to understand.

It can be very difficult to listen actively. It requires effort, as a host is generally doing many things at once: watching the clock, responding to notes from producers, keeping an eye on the script, checking available audio to see if there's a clip to use. Of all the tasks a host has to accomplish while on the air, the most important is listening. All other tasks are secondary. A great host is always a great listener.

MANAGE THE CLOCK

The reason so many interviews are pre-recorded and then edited for air on public broadcasting is that hosts and reporters don't want to manage the clock, or don't do it well. Making an interview come in to time is one of the most difficult things to do well, and reading this book won't teach you how to do it. Only practice, experimentation and discipline will do that, but I can offer you a few tips based on years of experience doing live radio.

It takes about 90 seconds, on average, to ask a question and get an answer. This is only a very loose estimate, but it can help you gauge how many questions you'll be able to ask. If it's a three minute interview, you only have time for the basics: who, what, where, when and why, and you'll have to decide what information you'll provide in your intro and questions and what your guest will supply. There's no time, generally, for follow ups, or indulging your curiosity. If you wander off target, you could miss some important information that's required to truly understand the story.

Otherwise, you can carry on with the interview as you like until you reach 60-30 seconds from the end. Remember, that's not 30 seconds from the end of the entire segment. You have to leave time to read your outro and promo the next segment. That generally takes a half minute or so. Most likely, your producer will give you a time cue. If not, you should ask her to give you two separate time cues: the first when you're one minute from the end of the interview and another 30 seconds later, leaving time for business afterward.

It's never good to interrupt your guest or cut them off to end the segment. It's best to avoid that, whenever possible. One of my strategies is to let them know before the segment begins that I might have to cut them off, and I tell them to watch for a specific signal from me (it's a twirling finger for me) that I need them to end their sentence. Obviously, that only works when the guests are in the studio with you.

You have to listen closely to your guest to know when to end the conversation. Listen to his pace, how long he takes to answer, and how often he breathes, places where you might be able to jump in. Let the guest know, when you ask the question, how much time is left if it's not a lot. If this person is long-winded, don't even try to make them answer in only 30 seconds. You should know quite early on if this guest can answer succinctly or not, and if they respond to your cues or simply keep talking regardless of your head nods and throat clearings and curt assents.

30 seconds is the benchmark. If you have 30 seconds left, make a quick decision. Can that person answer in half a minute? You should never leave the essential question of the interview until this point. Your essential question should be high up in the script, because it generally requires a long answer and at least one follow-up question. Don't ask an important question at the end. Aim for questions with simple answers.

If the guest says, "Well, let me explain something...", you can respond with, "Can you do it in 30 seconds?" That way, the audience is at least prepared for you to cut him off. It will likely come off not as rude, but as you're doing your job. If they start on a tangent, you can also say, "That is really interesting and we should have you back on to talk about that."

Just remember you're in control of the segment. We're talking about how to cut off a guest, but there are a lot of times when an interview is over and you still have several minutes left on the clock. Don't keep a conversation going after it's over. You'll lose the listener's attention and you probably won't get it back, at least not that day. This is one of the reasons I keep extra copy or short features on hand at all times. If an interview is over and I still have several minutes left on the clock, I simply read extra copy or slot in a short piece. Nobody wants to hear someone droning on to fill minutes. Don't put yourself or your listeners through that.

WRAP IT UP

In any show, even magazine shows, interviews are the core of the content. That's why I've taken so much time with this topic. No reporter or host ever really masters the interview: there's always room for growth and improvement.

Let's return to my running theme: preparation. Why is *Fresh Air* host Terry Gross so good? Because she prepares. Preparation means you can ask a question your guest has never heard before, and that's always a goal. That's what will distinguish your interview from the dozens of others the guest may have done.

Why are some interviews so boring? Let me count the ways. There are a number of possible reasons for this, but here are some common ones:

1. The host doesn't really understand the issue, or the host and producer didn't agree on the focus for the segment. That means the producer prepared one conversation and the host pursued a different one.

2. The host isn't interested. Some conversations may be important and engaging and unique and wonderful, but not right for your host or not right for

your producer. Know your host, know yourself, and be honest about what you do well and what you don't.

3. The host is *too* interested. If he or she is too knowledgeable about the topic, it can be too much inside baseball for the listener. This happens a lot with sports and politics. No one wants to feel like they're an outsider. Keep in mind that the purpose is not the host's enjoyment, but the listener's enlightenment.

4. The interview goes on too long. I talked about this a moment ago. Always be prepared with a Plan B so you can end a conversation when it's over and not when the clock tells you to end.

Another important part of preparing for an interview is listening to your colleagues. Listen to a whole variety of interviews with a critical ear, even the disasters, especially the disasters. Sometimes (unless the guest is a drunken James Brown, in which case, there's nothing you can do) you can identify the reasons why an interview went sour and try to avoid making the same mistakes. Listen to conversations and take note of the kind of questions that encourage people to reveal themselves.

To do better interviews, I can boil my advice down to three basic points: 1) Do your homework, 2) Focus on the guest 3) Listen actively. If you at least begin with those three things, you're on the right path to a good interview.

CARE FOR THE VOICE

For an industry that relies so heavily on the voice, broadcasting is remarkably uninterested in taking care of its pipes. Part of vocal pedagogy for a vocalist is learning to care for the voice, how to prevent damage to the vocal cords, how to maintain vocal health even during illness. If you are a broadcaster, then you are a vocalist. The more agile and healthy your voice, the more able you are to communicate emotion and information.

One of the biggest issues with the voice is most people ignore early signs something is wrong. It never fails to surprise me how little thought my colleagues give to the part of their body on which their career mainly depends. So, dryness in the throat is ignored. Discomfort or minor pain in the throat is also barely noticed, and post nasal drip is often untreated.

Why should you care about post nasal drip? Because the secretions that pool in your sinuses eventually ooze down the throat and over the vocal cords. That drainage causes the cords to swell, and that leads to all kinds of issues. The singer Adele had two hemorrhages that required surgery, and they began with a case of flu and a runny nose.

So, you should never allow post nasal drip to continue untreated. And those with allergies should be particularly vigilant. There are a number of ways to treat post nasal drip, including a sinus rinse (using a Neti pot, for example) or antihistamines. My director at *The Takeaway*, Jay Cowit, once gave me a ramekin of hot sauce to sniff during breaks in order to clear my sinuses (this works, but you'll need tissue on hand). However, it's best to see a doctor who can do a thorough examination and give informed advice and prescribe, if necessary.

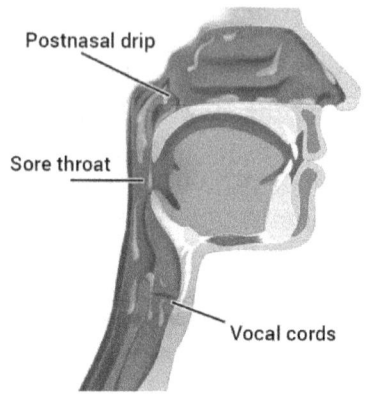

Illustration by Virginia Wilkerson

Do I really have to see a doctor for a stuffy nose? Yes! Explain to your doc that your career depends on your voice and you are looking for the best strategies for avoiding post nasal drip. The doctor most likely to take you seriously and offer useful advice is an otolaryngologist or ENT. ENT stands for Ear, Nose and Throat, and these physicians specialize in the head and neck. That's the doctor you want to see.

One of the most effective methods for maintaining a healthy voice is hydration. That means drinking lots of water and using a humidifier. I have a desktop humidifier under my computer monitor, and I drink between one and two liters of water a day.

Coffee is generally the beverage of choice in many newsrooms, but it's not very good for the voice. Why? Because coffee has a lot of caffeine and caffeine dries out your vocal cords. Nutritionist Sharon Zarabi says, "Caffeine pulls water out of your system and depletes the vocal folds of needed lubrication. Dry vocal cords tend to tighten which temporarily hinders voice range and endurance. The more caffeine you drink, the worse the effect on your voice."

That doesn't mean you have to give up coffee, but it does mean you should drink a commensurate amount of water to counteract the drying effects. Heck, water is good for you in all kinds of ways anyway, and you're mostly made of it, so why not?

If you need the coffee to feel alert and energized in the morning, consider using exercise instead. I visit the gym at 6am every morning, because it wakes up my mind faster than even espresso can. Even a brisk walk for a few minutes can have a big effect on your energy level. So, think twice before reaching for java.

There are a few other things you can do to take care of your voice, whether you're sick or not. First, don't smoke, and stay out of environments in which you will breathe a lot of secondhand smoke. You should also avoid screaming, whenever possible. So, if you tend to shout when you go to football games, be aware and try (at least try!) to resist the temptation to yell. As a voice major in college, I had to watch videos of what was happening in the throat when a person screamed and, believe me, it's not pretty. The same is true for singing loudly to music, as you might if you were at a live concert. You probably won't realize the damage you're doing to your voice until you wake up the next morning sounding like Harvey Fierstein.

Believe it or not, your posture can also affect your voice. If you tend to hold your neck in stressful positions, or clench your jaw, or grind your teeth, it can cause tension in your throat. Yoga is a perfect preventative for vocal trouble, as it also helps relax and deepen your breath.

Of course, you should get plenty of rest and have lozenges on hand at all times. Hosting is not a desk job; it's a performance job, and you should take care of yourself in the same way a professional singer does. I speak from experience.

Finally, if you notice something wrong in your throat, go see a doctor. You probably don't realize how small and delicate your voice box is. Here's the rule of thumb that I learned: imagine a nickel, then imagine drawing a triangle inside it, and then a line bisecting the triangle. That line is the size of your vocal cords, if you're male. If you're female, imagine a dime instead. These are tiny bits of tissue, and they need care.

Your voice is resilient, but much more easily damaged than you think. It's infinitely better to see an ENT and be told there's nothing to worry about than to ignore it, like Adele did, and end up on an operating table. Take care of your pipes! Without them, you're not a broadcaster, you're a mime.

STEP THREE: LET'S MAKE A SHOW

You have your host, you have funding, now it's time to create your show. Before you make any decisions about your format or focus or even theme music, you'll want to hire your staff. Why do the hiring first? Because the staff needs to be involved in all these decisions.

You want buy-in from everyone who's about to work very, very hard to get this show off the ground and on the air. Having the staff help form the show and understand the philosophical underpinnings will yield benefits during the first two years of production (which are the most difficult years, so you really need all the help you can get), and you want them on the same page.

STAFFING

Let me answer a few questions immediately:

Do you need an executive producer? Yes
Can the host be the executive producer? Yes
Should the host be the executive producer? Probably not.

Some hosts also make effective producers, but this structure only works when the show is host-driven and is a product of the host's vision. What's more, the host must be capable of deferring on some editorial questions.

Many shows have a host who is also executive producer. Al Letson of the *Reveal* podcast is both, as is Coy Barefoot, host of *Inside Charlottesville*. NPR's Guy Raz is host and editorial director for the *TED Radio Hour*. Glynn Washington is the host and executive producer of *Snap Judgment*. *The Diane Rehm Show* doesn't have an executive producer, but it does have a separate Managing Producer. So, hosts *can* be executive producers. Many organizations can't afford salaries for both positions and when it's a host-driven show, it can be better for the host to be the ultimate editorial voice.

Still, the host always needs someone who can advise and critique and say no, when needed. Even the most talented people don't have perfect judgment about their own performances. Without a qualified executive producer, your host is getting feedback from family or friends. That's not a good idea, not least because those people are mostly interested in what's best for the host, not the show. When the show is live, the host becomes the executive producer and senior editor while you're on the air. Otherwise, in the best case, you should hire someone to fill that role while the host focuses on hosting.

JOB DESCRIPTIONS

Let's begin with a list of job descriptions for the positions you may have on your show or podcast:

> Executive Producer – The Executive Producer is the final editorial arbiter on the show, although he or she isn't involved in day-to-day editorial decisions. What stories to do, which producer is assigned, what guests to book are all things the managing editor or senior producer can decide. However, if there's a difference of opinion between producers and the host, the executive producer steps in.
>
> S/he works with the host on the sound of the show, responds to listeners, and interacts with stations that carry the show. The EP should have the best ears on the team and listens carefully to make sure the show sounds as it should, that segments are balanced and fair, that music is appropriate. The EP works with various departments (engineering, IT, digital) to make sure the staff has the resources they need and know what is required of them.
>
> Jim Russell, known as the "Program Doctor", says this: "In a news or public affairs program, the EP is the principal journalist and needs to have very wide experience in journalism, knowing the rules, ethics, and practices of journalism as well as the laws and policies affecting the practice. He/she needs to

assure that the program meets the producing company's and other influentials' requirements of fairness, objectivity and balance. He/she needs to articulate production and journalistic standards and hold the staff accountable to them."

The EP also steers community outreach efforts for the show: when to do live remotes, when to ask the host to attend or speak at special events. The EP protects the host, makes sure the talent isn't overbooked. He/she also addresses editorial complaints from upper administration.

Director – The director works with the board op to make sure all clips are cued and the sound is good, chooses bumper music, and cues the host. The director is in charge of running the show while it's on the air.

The right candidate:

- Has 2 or more years working in LIVE radio environment (high pressure preferred)
- Is a quick digital editor with the ability to produce sound on the fly, during live broadcasts
- Understands radio clocks and ensures everyone in the CR adheres to the show's specific clock. In other words, if the show runs over time, it's the director's responsibility.
- Has experience working with talent, including coaching, editing, and communicating during show hours as well as during prep and post.
- Leads the Control Room environment firmly, while understanding the strengths/abilities of her or his control room

- Coordinates commercial/funder breaks and audio branding for segments, in cooperation with the Traffic Department
- Is responsible for all bumper music and break music
- Is responsible for quality of all on air soundbites, guest phone lines, in studio equipment
- Is able to respond quickly to change and adversity with reasoned decisions, delivered and rational instructions, all in a fast paced deadline-driven environment.

Board Operator/Audio Engineer

- Runs the board
- Edits audio
- Engineers and mixes pre-recorded segments
- Performs mic checks for guests and host
- Controls everything that leaves the studio

Line Producer – A Line Producer is in charge of the segments while the show is on the air. This person must have strong crisis management skills, make quick editorial decisions and have command of the Control Room. The line producer works closely with the managing editor to make sure the rundown is executable.

- Makes sure all guests are ready and comfortable
- Makes changes to rundown on the fly when required by technical difficulties, issues with guests or breaking news.
- Gives feedback to the host while on the air.
- Communicates with host about upcoming segments and sends extra copy that can be inserted. Generally, the line producer and director are the

only ones who talk to the host while the show is on the air.

<u>Managing Editor</u> – Acts as both assignment editor and staff manager.

- Handles the calendar, plans future coverage, and in collaboration with the Executive Producer, plans special events like debates, town halls, live performances.
- Maintains rundown
- Sends out notice to bureaus, promotions and News Director of upcoming shows and guests.
- Works with bureaus and the newsroom to collaborate on coverage.

<u>Editor</u>

- Edits all copy
- Works with producers to make sure the right guests are booked, segments are balanced, facts are correct
- Makes sure there is a consistency of voice/sound across all scripts for the show.

If it's possible, let the host *only* host, without reporting or editing on the side. As Jay Kernis says, "The best hosts sound as if they want to do nothing more at that moment than to be on that show and do that interview and find stuff out. Every day they come ready to be wonderful. What does it take for a staff to support that? That's a fundamental question."

THE EXECUTIVE PRODUCER

One way to support a host is hire an executive producer who's at least as smart as your host. The host needs someone listening objectively. Your host hears a very different show than what comes over the radio, and she needs to trust the person giving her feedback. Your host and executive producer need to have a good relationship, so the host can take constructive criticism and trust it's coming from a supportive place.

The executive producer handles the nonsense so the talent can focus on making sense. Jay Kernis says managers often accused him of coddling talent when he was producing, but the talent never complained. That's because, he says, he went to those meetings, he responded to the memos. He took the bullet so the hosts could focus and shine.

It's really a conflict of interest for the host to have a supervisory role. Often, when the host is in charge (except in rare cases), the show can become self-indulgent. It becomes a show about what the host is interested in and who the host wants to talk to. This is also how a show descends into what's called "host culture."

When the entire production serves the host and not the listener, it's a recipe for trouble and abuse. There should be an effective firewall between the host and the producers, and between the host and upper management. The executive producer is that firewall. What's more, the host can be a more effective mentor when not responsible for time sheets and promotions and the myriad meetings favored by radio stations.

Hiring the right executive producer is as important as hiring the right host. A great producer can develop a host, and turn mediocre talent into good talent. Your host needs a good producer. The executive producer needs to be willing and able to challenge the host and win.

What is Host Culture?

Perhaps one of the best descriptions of host culture was included in the CBC's investigation into Jian Ghomeshi's behavior while he was host of the show *Q*. Host culture is an environment in which deeply disrespectful behavior from a host is tolerated by management. That behavior can range from inconsiderate or annoying language all the way up to verbal (rarely, physical or sexual) abuse. Hosts are often given more latitude when it comes to conduct, and that can lead to exploitation. Common symptoms of host culture include: screaming, personal insults, fits of temper, and refusal to perform reasonable tasks.

THE REST OF YOUR STAFF

To do a one-hour, weekday show, you'll need a minimum five people, including the host. That is the bare minimum. The standard staffing is a host, an executive (or senior) producer, two producers and a board op. However, you also really need an editor and a digital/social media producer as well. You can't have two separate newsrooms; digital must be integrated from the beginning. The person who's creating digital content and social media strategy should be involved in each story from the onset. They need time to construct photo galleries, bonus content and web build-outs. There are many people able to explain the value of integrated digital content better than I, so I won't add to what's already been said.

It's possible to start with an editor and digital producer who work part-time. The same is true for the board op. Here's how I suggest you decide on staffing. Make a list of every task that will need to be done. Don't neglect even the smallest detail, like uploading stories to the web or calling guests to confirm dates and times. Then, estimate how much time it takes to accomplish each task. Add up the times, divide by an 8-hour day, and you'll know how many staffers you'll need. Overestimate on everything, as I can guarantee you will forget some tasks, and everything usually takes longer than you expect.

Stagger the start times of your producers, so someone is manning the phone from 7am until 6pm. Morning shows especially need someone to come in after the show is over to focus solely on booking for the next day. That way, you're covered in case of breaking news and last minute cancellations. Ideally, every producer needs at least one day when they're not on production, and can work on futures and get a break from deadlines and crises.

As I said, the minimum for a weekday show is five people, but they will work long hours. You can't sustain a workload like that, so make sure you have concrete plans to grow the staff. Or, make sure there is enough support from the rest of the newsroom and engineering departments to cover in times of need. I don't mean vague promises of support. I mean, create concrete protocols. How much content can reporters provide for the show? Who will cover for the producers when they're ill or on vacation? What engineer can board op and help with audio production? You must have answers.

Other staffing options include a part-time researcher and an acquisitions editor. The acquisitions editor finds suitable content from PRX, BBC Select, the Environment Report, and National Native News, among other sources. That person can also oversee features from reporters in the newsroom and freelancers, depending on their relationship with the News Director. What's more, she can track down special content for holidays and important anniversaries, or obituaries. It's also wise to train all of the reporters in your newsroom to produce. Diversification of skills can only help them in their careers, and it's immensely useful to have a deep bench.

KUOW in Seattle also has promo editors. Promos require a very different kind of writing than most journalists are used to, and it's important everyone understands that a promo is not a slice of the show. Its sole purpose is to capture attention and motivate people to listen. An intro to a segment might say: "Georgia Tech is now only the second university in the country to be certified as a Bee Campus. Students in the Urban Honey Bee Project help maintain hives and a 24-hour Bee Cam to raise awareness about the dangers threatening bee populations." But a promo might say: "Georgia Tech's mascot may be a wasp, but students' attention is focused on the school's resident honeybees." As Jeff Hansen says, promo editors "need constant attention to their writing, to ensure they don't fall back into clichés and old habits."

Remember: no matter how long or short the segments are, each requires the same amount of work from the producers and the host. They spend the same amount of time booking, writing, and researching.

You can't simply look at another station's talk show staff and duplicate the positions and job titles they have on their roster. Every station has different resources and a different culture, and it's often that culture that determines production style and workflow. In your calculations, you have to include technical capabilities, news reporters, and management support. In the end, your format and individual workplace dictates staffing. But as Jeff Hansen says, "A five-person staff can win awards. A seven-person staff is award-winning."

Once you have chosen your executive producer, consider bringing in a consultant who trains managers. A common mistake at public radio stations is a dearth of investment in training. Getting a right start is critically important, and training is worth the time and money.

WORKSHOP

> *Talent does not simply exist on its own. It has to be produced and edited. To me, talent cannot really be separated from content and format – it's sort of the holy trinity. The talent has to embody the content, the talent really has to be the content, and then that talent has to also be in a format, which brings out the best part of that person, so they're sort of inseparable. -- Doug Berman, Executive Producer, Car Talk and Wait Wait... Don't Tell Me!*

Now that you have your staff hired or at least planned, it's time to workshop. The audience research you did at the outset gave you some idea of the kind of stories your listeners want to hear, the kind of information they would find most useful, and what they think is missing from your station's existing programming. That's your starting point as you begin to plan your show.

During this process, it's helpful to remember what Jay Kernis calls the "ugly, unspoken thing in public broadcasting." Talk shows aren't entirely news. Talk shows and magazine shows are informed by the news, but they also have to include an element of entertainment. They should be as engaging and entertaining as they are informative. That means these shows shouldn't necessarily be overseen by the news director in the news department. In several of the places I've produced shows, I reported directly to the program director. This is something you might consider as well. It should be discussed early.

As you begin to imagine what the show will sound like, your goal in all your workshopping is to arrive at a definition of the show that is strong, precise, clear and has buy-in from everyone. The surest guarantee of mediocrity is to imitate what someone else has done. Don't try to be another show with a different host. Figure out who you are and what you do well, and do that.

One of the first and most important discussions you can hold when launching a show is about your purpose, your mission. Why are you doing this show? Is it to increase local programming, showcase a particular host, or highlight community events in your town? Why would the audience want to listen to this show above all the other options available to them? A sense of place – the place you are -- is your show's mission.

Put the management and production staff through this process together (and include upper management that may not be involved in day-to-day decisions). It's one thing to present a budget to your administration; it's another to include them in the workshop process so they understand why you are making certain editorial choices and budget choices.

Part of that early discussion should be which stories are local, and which aren't. Don't duplicate the rundown of *Morning Edition* or *Morning Joe*. The national conversation will take care of itself, and the major networks will cover it much better than you can. Excel in your own field. Focus on the local conversation and meet your community where it is. You can respond to the national conversation, as long as you're not repeating it. Make sure that people aren't dying or suffering down the street from you while you're finding a local expert who can talk about news in another city.

Don't worry about competing on specific stories. Put things on the air that have meaning to your listeners' lives, that help them meet and understand their own neighbors.

In the end, this show should be something you can't hear elsewhere. Jeff Hansen points out a common fallacy in local news magazines. He asks why stations spend resources covering a story that they've already spent money to buy coverage of from one of the networks. Spend those scarce local dollars on truly local stories. This holds true for podcasts as well. Don't do an okay job covering a story that someone else will cover using foreign correspondents and big-name experts.

I can't tell you how many local shows I hear that could be broadcast from anywhere in the country. Create a sense of place! Otherwise, listeners might bypass your podcast or show because they've already heard the story and your production values are lower than the network version.

Once you've settled on a mission and guiding principles for your show, create a list of bullet points and hang a copy at every desk. Here are the guiding principles we use at my show, based partially on those used by NPR's *Tell Me More*:

We're here to tell stories to our listeners that help them understand themselves and their world a little better. Our listeners challenge us to:
- Tell me something else;
- Tell me something I didn't know;
- Tell me something about the place I live;
- Tell me something that helps me understand other people;
- Tell me something that puts the news into deeper context;
- Tell me something I haven't heard before;
- Tell me something that I want to respond to;
- Tell me something that makes me care.

CREATE A FORMAT

Once you know what the show is about (the definition of the show) and the mission (the purpose), you can decide on a format. Will it be live or pre-produced? A straight talk show or a magazine? Will it include comments from listeners or not? Three 17-minute segments, four 12-minute segments or five segments of 10 minutes? What recurring segments will you have? Although many listeners hear the show in pieces and you should podcast all of the segments separately, remember you're not broadcasting a series of disconnected segments, but a complete show. You should forward promote everything in the hour at least once, and start your hour with a description of what the audience is going to hear.

Don't feel you're locked into a full hour. It's often best to start conservatively. If you can do 30 brilliant minutes, that's preferable to 60 good minutes. Also, remember that the format should serve the content, rather than the other way around. Be flexible so that stories that need more time get it, and those that should be short, are.

Often, stations will default to a talk show because it's the cheapest format option. But audience research tells us public radio audiences may not value local talks more than network shows, and the local shows are more expensive than most network shows. Once you factor in the salaries of all the employees needed to produce a local show, even a straight talk show, plus the equipment and other resources, any local show is an expensive proposition.

Jeff Hansen says he's no longer an advocate for talk shows. He says they often do more harm than good for a station. "Local talk shows are hit or miss," he says, "And mostly miss." Several of the experts I spoke to say public radio needs to get out of the talk show business. In the majority of cases, we don't do it well.

The same is true of podcasts. The top ten most downloaded podcasts of 2014 were, in order from top to bottom:

1. NPR's *Fresh Air*
2. *Stuff You Should Know*
3. *The Joe Rogan* Experience
4. *The Adam Carolla Show*
5. *This American Life*
6. *Radiolab*
7. *Freakonomics Radio*
8. *The Nerdist*
9. NPR's *Planet Money*
10. NPR's *Wait Wait...Don't Tell* Me

Every one of those podcasts is highly produced, with celebrities as regular guests. Other popular podcasts, like *Serial* and *TED Radio Hour* also have high production values. None of them sit a host down in front of a mic and let him or her jaw with relatively unknown authors, professors, politicians or performers.

That format is more the province of commercial radio, an industry that can spend half a million on a daily talk show and still show a profit. It's always better to focus on what you can do better than anyone else in your market. This is especially true now that the options have expanded so dramatically to include podcasts and internet radio and satellite radio and all the others.

The distinction between a talk show and a magazine show, besides the mix of produced reports with two-ways, is pacing. A magazine is generally five or more segments per hour. In a talk show, the interviews are longer, the segments are fewer. At KUOW, Jeff Hansen had a two-hour legacy talk show, and an afternoon talk show/magazine that he condensed into a one hour daily. In the first full year after making the change, he says, the station saw an 18% increase in listening at 9am and a 28%

increase at 10am, while airing national network shows at those times.

If you want to create a magazine show that matches the habits of most listeners, your format should resemble *Morning Edition*, which is about nine stories per hour. A faster pace often works best for news magazines during drive time because the pace is in closer alignment to the way people listen to radio. The average listening time these days is 10-11 minutes and people like to hear the beginning and the end of the stories they hear.

Longer segments can cause frustration because your audience has to step away before they hear the end. Jeff Hansen says when he changed format to include shorter segments, listenership of the local show went up 10%. You may not see the same results in your area; you'll want to do good audience research to figure out what your listeners prefer.

In the end, the sound and structure of your show are totally open. You don't need to follow any standards or preconceived ideas of how radio shows and podcasts are supposed to sound. For example, you could choose one host, one brand for the show. On the other hand, you could have a different host one day a week, someone who has very different interests and strengths, and can handle the topics your main host can't do as well. Think of this as the "Science Friday" design. There are many different options and none of them are necessarily wrong.

To make the best use of their original content, many stations produce every segment so it can be aired again. The stories can be excerpted for use on *Morning Edition* or *All Things Considered* or other network shows.

Be careful about scheduling special segments that hit at the same time each week: movies on Thursday, medicine on Wednesday, finances on Monday. Inevitably, you'll happen upon a week in which there's no news on that topic. If you're tied into a specific topic at a specific time, you'll end up having to produce a segment that's less important, that you wouldn't normally air.

However, regardless of the format you choose, remember that sometimes your listeners need a break from the tragic headlines of the day. Give yourself a little running room and breathing space. Certainly, you need to give listeners (and staff!) relief from the endless sorrow and seriousness of "important news." If you go from one serious, significant topic to another, the stories will lose impact and become monotonous. To paraphrase the movie "The Incredibles", if everything is serious and important, then nothing is. Break up the earnestness with some lighter topics. Create a diversified landscape.

As you create the architecture of your show, make sure you've built in forward promos. Let the listener know what the next 15 minutes will sound like. Let them see the underpinnings, so they feel they understand and can follow along.

I'm not including guidance on how to create call-in shows. As with anything, be cautious before choosing to launch a call-in show. Research has shown that airing live, unedited calls from listeners doesn't build community. Instead, it's very divisive and tends to drive away loyal audience members. Listeners complain about hearing personal opinions, especially when they're factually incorrect. If you do choose to take live calls from listeners, make sure you screen them carefully.

If the point of airing listener calls is to engage your audience and make them feel involved, or include them in your news making, there are other equally effective ways to do that. First, take calls, but record them so you can edit them before you air them. A well-staffed, national show like *The Takeaway* can do this while they're live on the air. If you're not live or your staff isn't large, you may want to allow calls to accumulate overnight and use them the day after.

Most shows will have to set up a toll-free number where calls can be recorded and downloaded later (Google Voice works well for this). Then, they can be edited like any other piece of audio and included in scripts. Use the same standards with these calls that you would any other clip. Don't let them run too long, don't allow callers to say inaccurate things without correcting them. You can also take responses from listeners via email, tweet, Facebook, or even Instagram and YouTube. If any of them are particularly good, you can call the listener and ask them to record them.

The most important thing to remember when deciding on a format is to be intentional, but flexible. Decide how you want the show to sound and then try to create that, beat-by-beat, minute-by-minute. If it doesn't work (and be honest with yourself), then be prepared to try something else.

SET UP YOUR SHOW: THE SMALL BUT IMPORTANT DETAILS

Here are just a few details about writing scripts (we go into this further in the Producer's Guide). First, when you're writing interview intros, never introduce two people at the same time. Give one person's name and title, and allow them to say hello before moving on to the next guest. Give the audience a chance to hear their voices, connected to their names. That will help them keep track of who's talking during the ensuing conversation.

When writing your promo, remember the promo is not the show; it's marketing. It doesn't have to have the same tone as the show, nor does it have to be serious or hard-hitting. The promo needs to be accurate, but its purpose is to entice and engage, to get people to listen to the show. It doesn't need to feature the most significant story of the day, just the most ear-catching.

Focus on placing forward promotes within the show so they look ahead to the next quarter hour. Don't surprise the audience. Forward promote often, and program the entire hour. Here are some templates from which you can build.

1. Rundown Template
2. Clip Sheet Template
3. Script Template
4. Guest List Template
5. Next Day Promo Template

RUNDOWN TEMPLATE

DATE:
HOST:
LINE PRODUCER:

SEGMENT A		TRT 20:00
9:00:00	Billboard	1:00
9:01:00	NPR News	5:00
9:06:00	[Slug]	13:30
9:19:30	Tease **(LIVE)**	0:30
9:20:00	First Break	2:00

SEGMENT B		TRT 17:00
9:22:00	B1 [Slug]	8:00
	B2 [Slug]	8:30
9:38:30	Tag + Tease **(LIVE)**	0:30
9:39:00	Second Break	2:00

SEGMENT C		TRT 17:30
9:41:00	C1 [Slug]	8:00
	C2 [Slug]	8:30
9:57:30	Show Close **(LIVE)**	0:30
9:58:30	Show Out	

CLIP SHEET   X/X/20XX

A SEG
CLIP1_SLUG_FILE#
IN:
OUT:
TRT:
"Blah, blah, blah..." - Transcription

B SEG
CLIP2_SLUG_FILE#
IN:
OUT:
TRT:
"Blah, blah, blah..." - *Transcription*

CLIP3_SLUG_FILE#
IN:
OUT:
TRT:
"Blah, blah, blah..." - Transcription

C SEG
CLIP4_SLUG_FILE#
IN:
OUT:
TRT:
"Blah, blah, blah..." - *Transcription*

CLIP5_SLUG_FILE#
IN:
OUT:
TRT:
"Blah, blah, blah..." - Transcription

SCRIPT TEMPLATE

Segment : [XX]   **SLUG**: [XXXXXXX]   [XX]
leads
Length: **Producer**:

Guest: (Name and title)
Location: (In studio, by phone-incl. number, ISDN, etc.)

INTRO:

QUESTIONS:
(Include bullet points/pre-interview notes here)

CALL OUT: (A question for the listeners about the segment like, "What do you think about this issue?" Plus, information on how to respond through phone, email, social media)

RESET:
If you're just joining us, my guest is _____ and we are talking about_____

OUTRO:
Include back announce of guest, call out to listeners, etc. Promo of next segment.

TAPE:
(Cut numbers, transcripts of bites that can be used)

BACKGROUND/ROLES:
What's the point of the interview, what roles will each guest play

RESEARCH:

(links, pre-interviews, etc.)

GUEST LIST   X/X/20XX

A SEG
Name (PHONE, STUDIO, ISDN?)
Title
Contact Info
Social Media

Name (PHONE, STUDIO, ISDN?)
Title
Contact Info
Social Media

B SEG

Name (PHONE, STUDIO, ISDN?)
Title
Contact Info
Social Media

C SEG
Name (PHONE, STUDIO, ISDN?)
Title
Contact Info
Social Media

Name (PHONE, STUDIO, ISDN?)
Title
Contact Info
Social Media

NEXT DAY PROMO

[Lead in...]

CLIP OF AUDIO – no more than 12 seconds
[Clip number]
IN:
OUT:
TRT:

[Identify audio, promo segment]

It's [name of show], [next day] at [time] from [your station or network].

It's [name of show], This morning at [time] from [your station or network].

EXAMPLE:

Quick, imagine a drug dealer in your head. I bet you didn't imagine a middle class white boy sitting in the living room of his parent's nice suburban home.

NDP_Drugs_05563
IN: *I'm gonna call some old college buds.*
OUT: *Some weed heads. Hit 'em up.*
TRT: 05

Inside the world of drug dealing that's outside the city.

It's *On Second Thought*, Monday at 9a.m. from GPB News.
It's On Second Thought, This morning at 9a.m. from GPB News.

Before you go on air, make sure you have a well-stocked shelf of evergreen material. You don't *want* to need emergency material, but you *will* need it. The importance of a well-stocked shelf can't be overstated. Having 6-8 segments ready to play when you need them will set your staff's mind at ease. It also ensures you're covered when a guest doesn't show or your host gets sick. Shelf interviews and music beds are your first aid kit for talk show emergencies.

BOOKING

> *Why this person on this topic at this time? You have to be able to answer all three questions. Post it on the wall, so you never forget. - Michel Martin, NPR host*

You've got a staff, a format, a mission and a whole slew of great stories that have been vetted through the pitching process. You're ready to start booking segments. This is the true test of your producers' skills.

Guests can make or break segments.

First, ask yourself if the story really requires an interview. On some days, the most important story requires no more than a headline, or an update of the current facts. There may be nothing to discuss, no nuances to explore or controversies to explain. Don't manufacture a conversation; if you don't need to talk to someone, make the segment a cut-and-copy or a brief, three-minute update with a reporter. If you can't think of a question that's surprising, then why book an interview?

Your first question when producing a segment should be, is there something here to discuss? The first couple of questions in any interview are usually easy to imagine, but what's the third question? If it's just information and details, with no nuance or analysis, doubt or pushback required, you probably want just 2-3 minutes with a reporter.

Do you need to hear multiple voices to understand the story? Does it require news gathering? Would it be improved with the use of ambient sound? If so, you probably want a reported piece and should assign a reporter to do a feature, if you can.

On the other hand, perhaps there is something in the story that's up for debate. Can you serve your audience by providing context, expert analysis, or reflection? Can you immediately think of five questions you want to know answers to? Then, it might be a great opportunity for an interview.

Have a conversation about booking as early as possible in the process of creating each show or podcast. Don't let your host walk up to the assignment board, or calendar where you plan upcoming segments, and be surprised by the guests who are booked. You may find you have to re-book. Keep the lines of communication open, keep the scripts updated with guest bios and focus statements, and make sure everyone is on board with the focus of your segment at all times.

The focus statement is supremely important. This is the answer to the question "why this guest at this time on this topic." It's the reason you're doing the story. I have my staff write a focus statement and include it in the script. If the focus changes, they change it in the script. That way, there's never a chance the focus will be lost or that there will be a misunderstanding about the segment's purpose.

Here's an easy way to teach people how to identify focus. Have everyone listen to an hour of *Morning Edition*. Have them all write down a focus statement for every segment they hear. Remember that you want to choose a focus that doesn't repeat the coverage people have already heard. The modern broadcasting environment, especially for podcasts, means listeners have almost infinite options, so don't duplicate.

You're aiming for "Huh, I never thought about it that way." Make sure your segment moves the story forward.

While you're doing this exercise with *Morning Edition*, also have your staff focus on one or two of the stories and explain what you really need to know in order to understand them. We often assume, in news, that people know certain things because *we* talk about them so much. We don't take a lot of time to explain the differences between Sunnis and Shiites, for example, or debt versus deficit, or how some judges run for office and some are appointed. The success of your stories depends on how well your listeners understand them when they're over. Could they explain it to someone else after they've heard your story? That's your aim.

Another important part of booking is diversity. Diversity doesn't just mean race, it also means gender, age, income level, education, religion, and all the other factors that make human beings different. If you do an inventory of your past guests and find most of them are male, white, educated and middle-to-upper-class, you have work to do. Don't issue a mandate or scold a person about booking choices; that's not a long-term solution. The executive producer and host have the power to change the culture if it's not serving your audience.

What does your community look like and sound like? Don't just book typical public radio and podcast guests (academics from elite institutions, experts from Brookings and other research institutes, hip tech entrepreneurs, pundits). We've done panels with all farmers, all local bloggers, all nerds and they've been very successful. They expand our contact list to include people we might not normally consult. Your show should reflect the multitude of perspectives and opinions in and around your community.

Sometimes, the host is an obstacle to diversity. Perhaps he's been in the business a long time and he has a long list of favorite sources. Perhaps she dismisses guests because they're not "articulate" or don't have impressive credentials.

This is why it's important to have an executive producer, or someone of equal authority, who's paying attention to the bookings. Someone has to have the authority to tell the host the show is not representative, and they are going to help the host fix that.

As I've said several times, every show should have a sense of place. In most cases, you don't want it to sound like it is produced in Anywhere, USA. To achieve a sense of place, you must establish criteria for your story choices, and stick to them. For example, don't choose an international topic like ISIS and say it's local because you've found a local expert. The topic should be local as well, not just the guest. Some people call this "distinctively local" as opposed to "merely local." Remember Michel Martin's mantra? Why this guest on this topic at this time?

That means you really shouldn't book people you think are bad on the air, just because you're having trouble finding anyone else. Booking is part of your editorial voice. Be intentional in your choice of guests, and be sure they can talk about the aspect of the story you're focusing on. Any interview you book should be about one thing. What is the essential question you're posing, from which every other question stems?

There's an unspoken idea in public radio that listeners care about certain subjects. We tend to return to the same general themes over and over again. The truth is, people will care about anything if you give them reason to. Our listeners are much more diverse in their interests than we think. I did one of the first NPR features on *World of Warcraft*, and didn't talk about the game as though it was a weird thing that pimply guys played in their parents' basements. That story got a huge response and I got dozens of emails from gamers thanking me for not portraying them as unemployed losers.

If you're trying to book someone remotely, in a town where breaking news is happening, try making cold calls to restaurants. A waiter can be a great source, someone who talks to all different kinds of people in the town every day. If you need to know how to pronounce a local word, call Denny's or the police station or even a local food pantry. If the story is overseas, you can call a university and ask to speak to international students to get both the correct pronunciation and their reactions. Be brave! Talk to regular people! While you have them on the line, ask them, "What are we missing about this story? What do people get wrong about your town?"

And don't forget to check inside your own building. You never know what kind of experience your colleagues have and where they've lived.

Correct pronunciations are important. They speak to credibility. Local people can ignore journalists who parachute in to cover a story, but you can secure their goodwill and get their help if you put in the effort to learn about them and their town. If you mispronounce local names, you lose those people. It can sound like you're mocking them, or think they're not important enough to research.

MANAGE THE STAFF

Working on a daily news show or a weekly podcast can be incredibly stressful. The staff needs to meet constant deadlines while maintaining creative energy. They're generally juggling a number of short-term and long-term projects at once, managing the demands of their editor, host and the guests they book. Producers are usually under pressure and overworked. Their work is under constant scrutiny, and they get a lot of criticism from multiple sources. They need to be healthy both mentally and physically, so they can work creatively.

It's important the entire staff know what's expected of them, and what they can expect from management. Before you launch the show or podcast, pilot it for a month. Jay Kernis suggests the following schedule for pilots of a weekday show: Week one, one show; week two, two shows; week three, do shows Tuesday through Friday and then on the following Monday, so that you get practice dealing with a weekend. Finally, in the fourth week, do a show every day. After each pilot, have the entire staff sit down and listen, then discuss. Management should listen as well and send notes privately.

Management should be intrinsically involved in the creation of the show and the establishment of its mission. Communication and feedback are the most valuable tools at your disposal. The staff needs to know how highly you think of them, or they won't be able to take criticism. And the feedback should come with what's called "noble intent," meaning it's totally sincere. No empty words. It's better to say nothing then pass along critiques that aren't fully considered and rationally based. Producers and hosts generally take criticism very seriously. They'll roll it over in their minds for weeks; they often dwell on it and worry over it. So don't give it lightly, and preface it with praise.

One of the most common managerial problems, mentioned by no fewer than two-thirds of the people I interviewed for this book, is that managers often don't recognize when someone is burning out. Managers sometimes neglect to ask how people are doing because the product is high quality and they assume everything is fine. Make sure managers have regular, active conversations, even when everything seems good, not just when there's a complaint or problem. People don't often feel empowered to call meetings, so management has to take the lead.

One warning sign of producer burnout is hearing the same guests (or people from the same organizations and schools) come on the show more than once. When producers are overwhelmed, they'll tap the same sources again and again. That means they're getting too many similar perspectives on stories and very little innovation. Overworked producers rely on the usual suspects. Listen for familiar names.

I don't recommend you put a lot of layers between the manager in charge and the staff. The executive producer should report directly to administration. The person who has the authority to make changes and solve problems should also be close enough to the content to know about significant upcoming coverage. A great manager is the best advocate for the show in the community, because she knows the show, knows the topics it covers and the guests it features.

If you are making decisions, you need to listen to the show and to comparable shows. You're in charge of people whose job you may not know how to do and, perhaps, have never done. So, ask questions about what other people do. Talk to producers and reporters at other public radio stations, not just managers.

Keep the lines of communication open, but don't just talk. Don't take notes in a meeting and then never follow up. The Society for Human Resource Management surveyed managers in 2013 and found that only 2% provide regular feedback to employees. Only 2%! Remember, a performance review doesn't count as regular feedback. Retreats are useless if nothing comes of them. If you meet the staff and ask for ideas, make a list and then take the top two ideas from the list and actually make them happen.

While I encourage managers to be involved in the production of shows, remember that the editorial firewall has to be absolute. If the administration has a complaint about an editorial choice, someone on the staff should be designated to listen to and address those issues. The ideal person is the executive producer, so that the person taking these complaints is not involved in day-to-day editorial decisions. The E.P. of a large staff is mostly an administrator. In many cases, though, the staff won't be large enough to have a manager who's not involved in day-to-day decision-making about stories and sources. So the designated person must be scrupulous in separating discussions with upper management from editorial vision.

In that case, you might choose the next manager up the chain, like a Program Director or VP of Radio. It's vitally important that person be a trained journalist who listens to the show and can put complaints into context. If your show or podcast is to maintain credibility, there can't be an appearance of undue editorial influence from upper management. Imagine the host of your show being asked, at a public event, whether the GM or CEO interferes with reporting. Construct a system that lets your host answer that question honestly.

Since we're back to your host, let's talk about how to manage a host. Both the host and the executive producer, if they're separate people, should have veto power. This is how you manage away from "host culture."

One of the first questions to ask is, "Who says no to the host?", Your host needs someone to protect them from themselves, someone who has his back. That can't be imposed, though. You can't order a host to do something they don't want to do. It should be a relationship that evolves.

If something goes wrong, if a fact is incorrect, or a guest complains about unfair treatment, or there's blowback over a story, the host is blamed. It's the host's name and credibility on the line. We make a bargain with our hosts. The trade-off is we don't make them say something they don't want to, and we don't make them do an interview if they absolutely refuse to do it. If your host is refusing stories all the time, then you have a problem. But under normal circumstances, you can't and shouldn't strong arm the talent.

One of the best ways to manage a host is to offer training and development. People invest a lot of money finding the right host, then often totally disconnect and walk away. Maintain your host like your house or car. Do regular check-ups.

Perform regular maintenance. Don't wait for a problem. Just as with the producers, everything is not okay because things sound good on the air. Every two weeks, schedule a meeting with the host and ask, "Do you have everything you need?"

The host needs to know someone has her back. It's the host's name and career on the line, and she needs things to work. A good host is emotionally connected to the work, so she cares when things go awry. And that can make a host emotional. When hosts complain, they like to know they've been heard and acknowledged. Look for a strong manager who's authentic, invested, and trusted by your host. Hosts are reassured when they know someone is listening closely, and checking numbers and facts in real time.

The manager who oversees the show should listen to it every day, and carefully. Take notes! Don't stop the host from trying things. You'll get better results if you encourage experimentation and innovation, so don't be afraid of risk. But if something fails, name it. Be honest, without shaming the host or the producers.

Management gets in the way if they're not willing to experiment, and are only concerned with getting the show on the air. Managers sometimes don't have a high threshold for mistakes. But when you're creating something new, things won't always work, and that's okay. If you create a safe space for your staff, you will also provide a creative work environment.

Your hosts are only as good as the staff who support them. So the relationship between them is vital. The staff needs to feel valued and trusted. It's true, you may encounter ego issues on the part of your host. But that's not what's going to cause issues for you. Hosts become difficult when no one protects them from making a mistake on air, when the facts were wrong or a pronouncer was incorrect or a guest doesn't show up.

The host is completely reliant on his staff. It helps if the host is invested in the staff's morale. From the producers' point of view, the host gets to talk to interesting people, he gets all the glory and attention, while the producers are working long hours without recognition or other benefits. So, the host should be sensitive to the mood among the staff and work to make sure that communication is clear and everyone feels supported.

The best show is the product of wonderful producers with great talent. Have frequent conversations about expectations. It's not a subject that's ever settled permanently; you'll have to return to it again and again. Have everyone explain what they need from each other. Survey the team often and ask specific questions: When does the host sound best? What interviews could have gone better? What went wrong? Was it the fault of prep or hosting? This should be part of regular listening sessions.

If there's serious conflict between staff members, set up mediated conversations with the host, producers and an unbiased third party. If that doesn't work, you may have to consider separation. People often fire themselves. The company hires them to do a specific job and sometimes people decide they don't want to do that job anymore. You will know pretty quickly if a host will work or not. Give it six months, no longer.

On a side note, guest hosting is a good place to recruit new talent. Give your guest hosts some freedom. Give them some autonomy to show intellectual leadership. Do they have an ear for pacing? Do they have a sense of a story arc? Without that, it's like getting into a car with someone who doesn't know where they're going. Where are you taking me and all the listeners?

Guest hosts should have a natural sense of direction on the air. Ask yourself, can I follow what's happening? Do I feel satisfied at the end? These are the kinds of things you're looking for. Make use of the days when you have a guest host. Instead of seeing your permanent host's vacation time as a burden, view it as an auditioning and recruiting opportunity.

In the end, managing a host isn't the biggest challenge when you're producing a show or podcast. Transparency is. All too often, management in broadcasting makes the mistake of keeping things secret for as long as possible. The truth is, whatever it is you're hiding is probably not a secret. When things are unsaid, rumor fills in the empty space. It takes a lot of communication to put on these shows and have them succeed. You are dealing with highly intelligent journalists. They notice when something is going on, and they're often relentless in ferreting out the details. It's better to have the information come from you than for it to be relayed in whispered conversations throughout the building.

There are often a lot of unsaid things at a station, and why systems are set in stone is one of the topics people avoid talking about. If someone asks why changes can't be made, people dodge the discussion by saying: "This is the way we do it here. This is the way we've always done it." Those phrases are the enemy of most innovation. Unless you're talking about public radio's core values or ethics of journalism, anything should be subject to change.

LISTENING SESSIONS

Listening sessions are really important. I'm not entirely sure why, when our core business is creating an audio signal, so few managers sit down to listen to the content with staff and discuss it.

The best way to make a show or podcast better is to schedule time to listen to the work you've already done. Call it a listening lounge, make it informal, bring coffee and snacks so there's no fear and people will speak honestly. Hold it with producers sometimes and with talent other times It's not a great idea to hold a listening session in which everyone listens to an interview and starts critiquing the host or vice versa.

I have producers bring in any audio they want, including other shows and music, if they think they've found something the team can learn from. You want lots of smart feedback, so also ask your interns to analyze the show.

It's also a good idea to build sessions around a specific theme or focus. For example, just listen to show opens, resets or forward promos. You can also take excerpts of segments and discuss topic selection and guest selection. Focusing on individual show elements can be more productive and produce more specific ideas than trying to listen to whole shows.

FAQ (COMMON PROBLEMS)

There are a few issues that arise on almost every show or podcast. Some are big and complicated, some are simple and easy to fix. But chances are, if you produce a show for longer than a year, these things will come up and it's wise to keep an eye and ear out for them.

1. Long intros - This is what Ellen McDonnell points to as the most common mistake. "Long intros are the kiss of death," she says, "Get to the point." Intros should last about 20 seconds until you introduce a guest or start the feature. Learn to curb your genius. Also, don't let the last line of the intro contain the same information as the first line of the piece, which is to say: don't repeat yourself. It always sounds sloppy.

2. Topics that don't reflect the news of the day - This happens when shows are booked in advance and producers don't want to dump the work they've done and re-book an entire show. The result? A huge headline is happening in your community and you don't cover it properly. You have to bump guests for news.

This will happen, so expect it. You can't expect the listener to care about a non-urgent story when there's real news happening. Radio (even if it's streamed) is all about immediacy. If your show sounds irrelevant, your audience will turn to another source. You are not just competing with other radio stations and TV, but also podcasts and HBOGo on tablets. The strength of audio broadcasting is its ability to reflect the current moment, so don't let your show be always talking in the past tense.

3. Bad guests - You can tell producers on a show are rookies if the guests haven't been pre-interviewed. Often, producers will book local reporters and assume they will be okay on the air. But many local reporters aren't media savvy at all. Your producers have to train guests to sound great. (You'll find instructions on how to do this in the following Producer's Guide.) Local guests are great because they're fresh voices with compelling stories and they sound genuine because they're authentic. But it takes time and training to make them sound polished.

4. Uneven performance - Jeff Hansen says this is the number one indicator that the show is under resourced. If the show is hit or miss, then you probably need more staff.

5. Bad clips - Producers will sometimes pull clips they find interesting but don't hear them from the listener's point of view. So, you'll hear bites that end with upcuts or have awful sound quality, or are really boring or too long. The attention span for audio is 20-30 seconds maximum. If you can keep it below ten seconds, that's even better. Short bites, not big mouthfuls.

6. Inside baseball - This is especially common when the host knows the guest well. The audience doesn't care

about personal anecdotes from the host. They don't care when the host last saw the guest, or how her kids are doing. This also occurs when the host knows the subject matter really well. I've heard local political shows that sounded like a bunch of political operatives sitting down and BS-ing in a bar. Everyone in the studio may enjoy it, but you've left the audience out. Listeners don't want to feel like an outsider, so avoid conversations with "insiders." Don't talk shop.

7. Chaotic Roundtables - Roundtables are often a mess. They are generally used as an easy way to address the news of the day, but roundtables require *more* planning, not less. Hold a planning meeting for the segment and make sure there are guests from all necessary points of view. You also have to pull plenty of audio, so that it's not a solid block of people talking. And like any other segment, make sure the roundtable has a beginning, middle and end. It's awful when you just gather a bunch of people in the studio and meander from topic to topic. Create a structure.

8. "Host culture" – (See the inset in the section on staffing.) This comes up frequently. Sometimes the complaints about talent are unfounded, sometimes they're legitimate. Make sure you do some investigation when there's a complaint and verify the source of the problem. There are rare cases when a host is terrible to work with and should be let go. Most of the time, if a host is acting badly, it's because the host feels unsupported. Perhaps mistakes were made and not addressed. Perhaps the host feels scared, for one reason or another. Investigate and try to address the real cause of the problem, not just surface issues.

THE BIGGEST PROBLEM

In doing research for this guide and talking to people from all over the country, all of those issues came up. But the number one complaint about local shows is that they're boring. Now, boring is a vague descriptor. I tried to drill down and get my experts to explain what they meant when they said, "boring." Here's what I learned about the causes of "boring."

1. Dull, uninteresting interviews - There are a number of reasons for this, but they all generally boil down to this: no passion. It could be your host is just reading questions off the page and not really listening. Perhaps the guest is repeating the same information we just heard in the newscast, without offering new insights. Sometimes it feels like a box is being checked and an interview is happening because the producers think it's obligatory. There's no passion, nothing to get excited about, no tension. Any story that you put on the air needs tension to capture attention.

2. Guests Go On and On and On - Often, local hosts try not to interrupt the guests. But interruption is the only method you have for steering the interview, beside your questions. Guests take over when the host is not entirely in control. It's a skill to be able to interject without being rude. Redirect the guest by saying, "I hear you saying this...." and then turn to another point. If they're not responding to the questions, be a human being in your response! Say, "That's interesting, but it's not the question that I'm asking." Don't let the guest control the interview.

3. Lack of Preparation - Some of this echoes what I said before about pre-interviews. Remember, it's not only about whether the guest has a good story; it's about whether you can get them to tell that story. If guest isn't a great talker, be prepared with a lot of great clips to help move the segment forward. Do research into both

the topic and the guest. Nothing shuts down a guest faster than having to answer the same question he's answered a hundred times before.

4. Host Doesn't Care - Sometimes your host doesn't have buy-in on the segment. That's a recipe for disaster. Hosts need to be genuinely curious about a *lot* of things and it's not usually difficult to spark their interest. So, find a way to make things interesting. What's the question you don't know the answer to or can't guess? People can hear if you don't care. So if the host really isn't into the story, kill the segment. You can't force it on the host. You have to convince the host to buy in, or let it go. But you must do that before it gets on the air.

THE PRODUCER'S GUIDE

Great producers are truly rare, but strong producers can be developed. Unfortunately, much like hosts, we often hire people and set them to their tasks without training them, informing them of expectations (expectations are not the same as deadlines), or investing in the development of their skills. That's why I wrote this Producer's Guide, so my staff would have a guide they could turn to regularly for advice on pitching, booking, writing, pulling audio and editing.

This guide is designed to stand alone, to be printed and distributed as needed. As with anything in this book, feel free to use the content as you need, but remember to attribute the material. I've included wisdom from many different brilliant people in this guide, and they deserve credit.

This is the producer's guide I present to my staff at Georgia Public Broadcasting in Atlanta. Feel free to personalize it for your workplace and your staff. For example, in the section called "The Basics of the Job," the first paragraph lays out how I like my scripts to be written. You'll need to change that to match the preferences of your host. Just remember that the live script is meant to serve the host.

PRODUCER HANDBOOK

Celeste Headlee

GUIDING PRINCIPLES

1. We are here today to make an audio signal - David Candow

At heart, that's what we do. All other considerations are secondary to the quality of the sound. That doesn't mean just high-quality audio. It means the entire audio product, including content, voices, music, and effects, should be the best audio product you can make. An audio signal is specifically designed to be heard.

2. The best story, not the best headline

Our jobs exist within a broader universe of news coverage. Americans get their news from all kinds of sources, and there is no need to present a slightly different version of the same story they got from 3 other places. Short of a 9/11 size event, there's no such thing as a story that we "have to cover". Did you ever hear a cover version of a song and think, "That's sounds almost exactly like the original. Why did they bother?" Well, we don't make bad covers.

3. Diversity that reflects the local area

This topic will be addressed several times in this handbook, but it bears repeating as often as possible. The US has nearly 320 million people. More than 80% of them live in cities or suburbs, 51% are female, more than 12% are black, 5% are Asian, 16% are Latino, 3% are mixed race. Those demographics will shift even further away from European ancestry in the years to come. But already there are a lot of interesting people out there who are not both white and male. Let's find them.

4. No pundits

Make sure all of your guests have a real job beyond talking and writing books. A pundit is an expert in a particular subject or field who is frequently called on to give opinions about it to the public. If that's all they do, we're not interested. As Doug Mitchell said, "We have to continue to insist that we grow the art form that is talking to people who are different from ourselves. Echo chamber journalism is not journalism. Talking only to people with whom we are most comfortable leads to inaccurate storytelling and a sheltered, if not uninformed, consumer."

5. Topics that feature real people doing/saying things that can affect others

We don't find a group of people doing odd or quirky things and then talk about how quirky they are. Someone in the story has to be actually doing something, and it should be more interesting than just being "really different from us." Cover a story, not a type of person.

6. Every segment should include an element of surprise

It's always there. Find it. I'm not talking about earth-shattering new information. If someone thinks "I've never heard that before" or "I've never thought of it that way before," that's enough. But if they basically know everything they're hearing, why are we doing the segment? Leave the updates for headline news.

7. Radio is people talking to people about people

Even if it's a recent study, an economic indicator or a new law that's been passed, it's still about people.

8. We are never done learning - never turn down training

Someone with 20 years' experience may be someone with two years of the same experience 10 times over. Don't stagnate. Never turn down free training and always try to branch out into areas you've never touched on before. Learn engineering, learn Spanish, learn about the environment, take up the balalaika... just keep learning.

9. We do not attempt to create false balance

Never book a guest whose opinion is fringe opposite a guest whose opinion is either mainstream or backed by the weight of scientific opinion. In other words, we do not put Bill Nye against a Tea Party candidate on climate change and we do not pit Neil DeGrasse Tyson against a flat-earther. You can feature a climate change denier, but never imply their position is equal in credibility or based on fact. Stick to the guidelines of the *BBC Trust*.

THE BASICS OF THE JOB

1. Every script should include an intro, outro, bullet points of information and/or suggested questions (see templates above). Note any significant or surprising facts. The producer should also write promo copy for the segment and include the guest's contact information. Do not spend a lot of time on the questions. Include them only to give a suggested arc of the conversation and/or topics on which the guest is particularly good or lively. Your host will generally not read those questions as written; they do not need to be edited. What she needs is the arc of the conversation, important facts she should know, takeaways from the pre-interview.

2. Booking guests - Here beats there. We always try to get guests in the studio, rather than on the phone or Skype. Press them on this if they're within driving distance. Make sure they understand people are much more likely to pay attention to what they're saying if the sound quality is good. Bad phone sound makes people tune out. However, we prefer the right guest with less-than-perfect sound to a second tier guest in studio. The right guest is both a good talker and an expert.

How do you know you have the right guest? From your pre-interview. Of course they speak well, but what are their best stories? What do they say that makes you think, "Wow, I didn't know that." You just need to give the host enough to know what to ask about. You don't want them to spill everything in the pre-interview ("It's like I told your producer on the phone…"). Hold it for air!

3. NO PUNDITS. Every guest must actually do something besides talk and write books. A professor is fine because he/she teaches in addition to talking/writing. A columnist is okay if they are also a journalist, but don't book people who USED to do something and now just talk. Exceptions, of course, are people who used to do something really, really

significant, i.e., former presidents, former Popes, former Secretaries General of the UN.

4. Follow the broadcast writing guidelines included later in this guide.

5. We don't do profiles unless it's a current newsmaker or someone who just died. Every story we book must have a compelling reason for talking about it right now. That includes music (newly released album?), book (just published?), theatre (just won a Tony?), politics, or economics. An interview needs insight and tension. You're not aiming to be a definitive guide, but an engaging tour guide. It needs to be deeper than what the listener can read in Wikipedia but not a master's thesis.

6. We don't chase press releases, even when the press release is about a new study. There are probably tens of thousands of studies being conducted by prominent universities at this moment. They are not all news. If we are going to cover a study, it's because there's an element of surprise in the results and/or it relates to a current news item.

7. We should have two independent sources on any news item before we call it "verified." Unconfirmed is a word we rarely use.

8. Do not slaughter the great in search of the perfect. When editing an interview, use a light touch. If a segment is too clean, too sanitized, too "perfect", it sounds like the Saturday Night Live version of public radio. You can leave stumbles. They enhance the conversational tone. Don't be afraid of LIVE RADIO. Live radio is exciting, with its own unique energy. And don't be afraid of transparency about mistakes, either. For example, "We asked a question yesterday and only got one response. So clearly, that was the wrong question to ask. Let's try again." Or, "We did a segment yesterday about guns in libraries and most of you think we missed the real issue. So

let's return to the topic and this time, talk with someone from…"

9. We want our guest bookings to reflect the diversity of the community and the country around us. If the show is 75% white males, then we have failed. We should always aim for an even split between men and women, plus a diverse group racially who are not there as representatives of their race. In other words, don't book two white males to talk about politics, plus a woman to comment on Hillary Clinton's possible candidacy and a Latino to react to the latest immigration story. NOTE: your host doesn't count toward diversity in the segment.

10. Be sure to coach your guests. Remind them to answer the question in their response, rather than come prepared with things to say. Keep it brief, don't use technical terms or acronyms, and if they hear the host trying to interrupt, stop talking.

Is the guest pumped up with enthusiasm before they go on? Coach them before they go on, but don't talk to them about the subject of the segment. "I've spoken with you, this is an important conversation. I know you're passionate about this. We need to hear that passion on the air." Instruct your guests to speak up, speak loudly and don't hold back.

Jeff Haden wrote a great guide to being a better on-air guest. You can find it in *Inc.com.*

11. You have to call every guest before the show to make sure they're up and ready for the interview or on their way into the studio. When they arrive, greet them, and offer coffee or water. Chat with them to relax them, but don't talk about the subject of the interview.

12. Every team member is expected to bring 2-3 pitches to the table every day. It doesn't matter if the pitch isn't accepted, just pitch. Every pitch should be presented with a focus

statement: why this guest at this time on this topic? Also, what's the golden moment the producer is aiming for: what moment will be totally unique in this segment? Where's the surprise? Expect pushback when you pitch stories. Here's how it works: you bring a pitch to the meeting, you may argue back and forth with the host or other producers, and the pitch will either be shot down, or you'll convince the host to do it.

13. Provide pronouncers

I can't emphasize enough how important pronouncers are on a live show. For a pronouncer, every syllable is separated by a dash and the one that's emphasized is in all caps. So my name would be – suh-LEHST HEHD-lee
Common pronouncers are:

- A: ah (father, arm), a (bat, apple), aw (raw, talk), ay (fate, ace)
- E: ee (feet, tea), eh (get, bed), ew (few)
- I: eye (time, ice), ee (machine,), ih (pit, middle)
- O: oh (note, oval), ah (hot), aw (fought), oo (food, two), u (foot), ow (how, clout)
- U: ew (mule, hue), oo (rule, fume), u (put, curl), uh (shut, pull)
- Consonants: g (got), j (general), k (keep, cat), ch (chair, butcher), sh (machine, shut), z (disease, visit)

Take a look at this NBC Pronunciation Handbook. It may be old, but most of it is still viable.

SUGGESTIONS FOR STAYING HEALTHY

1. Don't sit at your desk all day.
Seriously. Good research shows it's really bad for your health and puts a damper on your creativity. Walk to lunch, walk around the building, read scripts while pacing. Just get up and move from time to time. A relevant quote from a piece in the

New York Times: "Employees who take a break every 90 minutes report a 30 percent higher level of focus than those who take no breaks or just one during the day. They also report a nearly 50 percent greater capacity to think creatively and a 46 percent higher level of health and well-being. The more hours people work beyond 40 — and the more continuously they work — the worse they feel, and the less engaged they become."

Leave the building for lunch. Only 1 in 5 Americans leaves their desk for lunch. The fact is, taking frequent breaks improves a person's focus and makes him/her more productive. So, go get coffee or better yet, go stare at a tree. Researchers have found that "performance on memory and attention tests improved by 20% after study subjects paused for a walk through an arboretum."

2. Don't try to multitask.
Focus on one task at a time. This is difficult for producers who are juggling multiple stories and guests, but the key is to focus on one of them at a time. Work on one story with all your attention, then set it down and move to something else. From *Forbes*: "When you're trying to accomplish two dissimilar tasks, each one requiring some level of consideration and attention, multitasking falls apart. Your brain just can't take in and process two simultaneous, separate streams of information and encode them fully into short-term memory. When information doesn't make it into short-term memory, it can't be transferred into long-term memory for recall later.
If you can't recall it, you can't use it. And, presumably, you are trying to learn something from whatever you are doing, right? Instead of actually helping you, multitasking works against you. It's making you less efficient, not more."

3. Keep a notebook/diary with a record of what you did that day
Taking stock is shown to increase productivity and reduce stress. Just keep a notebook open and jot down each task you do, or maintain your list on your computer.

4. Go out and do stuff.
Don't work a long day, then go home and turtle on your couch with a frozen dinner. Again, we have good research that shows forcing yourself to get out and go to the bar with friends, have dinner, see a movie, meet people and socialize, reduces your stress and makes you more efficient. Have a hobby. It never hurts to read a good book.

5. Don't sacrifice your health for the job.
Be the healthiest person you can be. Sleep enough, eat good stuff, exercise. No story is worth killing yourself. This is a stressful job. Acknowledge that, and find ways to reduce your stress level. Stand in a stairwell and scream if it helps you.

HOW TO PRODUCE A SEGMENT

Let's walk through one segment, step by step, to show how it's usually done. There are, obviously, exceptions to every rule. But this is the standard, plus tips on being the best and most efficient producer you can be. Don't discount shortcuts, by the way. Some of the advice below is designed to make you quicker and more productive. For someone who is constantly on deadline, feeding the beast of a regular show or podcast, the ability to work quickly is an invaluable skill.

1. PITCH A STORY

Most shows and podcasts hold pitch meetings. Or they at least meet regularly and talk about what's going to be on the next show. It's tempting to see interesting headlines and pitch stories that you don't know much about. Don't do that. It's a waste of everyone's very valuable time.

Instead of bringing five unresearched pitches to the meeting, bring one or two good ones that you're prepared to fight for. Your colleagues, including the host, may push back on the idea. If you're passionate about it, argue back. Present your case for the story. That back-and-forth is an important part of the editorial process.

A pitch is generally three or four sentences, containing the essential information needed to decide whether a segment is worth doing. There are a few key elements: a focus statement, sources, audio possibilities, deadline, and some links to more details or supporting information.

The Focus Statement
Why this guest on this topic at this time? This focus statement may change as you work on the piece, but it should always reflect the compelling reason for doing this story right now. For

example: "Kelly Gissendaner was executed last night at a prison in Georgia. Why did she lose her final appeal?"

Key Sources

Who would we talk to for this piece? What would they tell us? What kind of nuance or context can they offer? For example: "We can talk to the reporter who's covered her case for two decades, plus a legal expert to explain how death penalty cases work differently in Georgia than almost anywhere else."

Audio Possibilities

Can you collect ambient sound? Is there music? What about clips from other sources? Vox (non-narrated audio from various sources) from people in the community? What will this piece sound like? For example: "I have audio from people around the state, giving their reactions to Gissendaner's execution. We also have a short clip of her speaking in court, and a clip from a family member of the victim."

Deadline

Is this story pegged? If so, what date does it need to run? Even if it's about a concert happening three months in the future, you should include the expiration date on your pitch. For example: "Gissendaner was executed last night. This story should run by Tuesday or it may sound dated."

More Details

At the bottom of your pitch, include a link to the story that caught your eye, or any other information you might think would flesh out the story. If the pitch is accepted, this is the first place your editor and host will look to start doing research.

2. START YOUR SCRIPT

As soon as a pitch is approved, create a script. Immediately copy your pitch, including links and other information, into the script. Your editor or senior producer can help you choose a slug. The slug, or title, of your piece is important as that's what others will search for when trying to find the script. Slugs must be uniform.

You should update the script constantly. Don't keep notes elsewhere and wait until the day before to post in the script. Your script is a living document. Save your notes there, as well as transcripts of pre-interviews. If you're sick and someone else has to step in, they should find all of the relevant information there. The host should be able to open the script at any time and see the focus statement.

The staff on shows and podcasts juggles a lot of different stories. Inevitably, someone will look at the board and ask, "What is that story about?" The script should always answer that question: here's the focus, here's the peg, here are the sources we're using, and here is the audio we want to pull.

I've included a script template earlier in the book, but you should talk with your host about what he needs on the script. It's a pact that producers make with talent. The host says, "I need you holding the net so I can walk across that wire." And the producer asks, "What do you need to do your job best? What gets in the way? How can I help you?"

Maybe your host likes all of the research for segments printed out and handed to them in a file folder. Maybe she likes everything to be emailed to her. When your host finishes an interview, check with her and see that everything is laid out as she wants it. Does she want a separate sheet of guests' names and titles, as I do? I also like a separate clip sheet, so I can keep the script open on my computer and look for a specific bite on a separate page. The goal is to make the information as fast and easy to find and read as possible, so the interview goes smoothly and sounds polished.

3. BOOK A GUEST (THE PRE-INTERVIEW)

Your process for booking will be unique to you, but here's how I do it and how I teach others to.

First, decide what voice you're looking for and what you want them to bring to the segment. Think about this carefully! Say you're doing a story about a significant rise in housing prices. That may seem like a straightforward piece that just requires an economist to give the numbers. But how will it sound different if you book a realtor instead, or someone trying to buy a house, or a loan officer? What if you found an economist who studies wealth and the connection to property? Study the focus statement, figure out what questions you want to ask, and decide what sources are most likely to have the answers.

Once you know, in broad strokes, who you're looking for, cast a wide net. I usually put out emails to universities in my area, plus a posting on ProfNet, plus a quick look through sites like SheSource.org and the Rainbow Source Book at Poynter. Be as specific as possible in your posting. If you're looking for an economist who can compare your local numbers with data in other states, then say that. The more specific you are, the more time you'll save.

Your staff should keep a contact list of sources you've used, with notes on each person. What are their areas of expertise? Keep good notes on the guests you use. This will also save a great deal of time.

Booking a celebrity is a different proposition altogether. First of all, you'll often have to work your way through a phalanx of managers, agents, promoters or PR agencies.
In their minds, they're doing you a favor, and they often expect you to accommodate them.

If you're having trouble getting the celebrity's people to call you back, try reaching out to the venue where he or she will be performing. The venue (concert hall, theatre, university) has a lot more invested in getting promotion for the event, so they can be really helpful in booking.

Also, be prepared for the celebrity to be late, sometimes more than an hour late, or to flake out. No matter how many times you confirm with a publicist, celebrities will often let you down. Make sure you have a backup plan, just in case.

If you're doing the interview as a pre-record, I don't recommend scheduling it late in the afternoon. One Academy Award-winning actress was nearly two hours late to an interview, and the producer booked it for an hour after the host normally goes home. That means the host didn't start the interview until three hours after she was supposed to go home. She was exhausted by then, and irritated, and that's not a great way to get a good interview.

Before you invest that kind of time and energy into the interview, though, make sure it's worth it. Celebrities will always try to claim an outsized portion of your time, by asking for multiple accommodations. In my career, there have been many times that my staff has busted butt to make a celebrity interview happen and people have stayed late, only to have the person flake out or give a terrible interview anyway.

In the end, it's not worth it unless the person is a real get. While it may be cool for the staff to book a "name", you may not get a benefit with listeners that's equivalent to the effort you put in. Don't mistake your own excitement at meeting someone famous with the value of the eventual segment. A selfie ain't worth it.

I'm not saying don't bother booking celebrities. A good interview with a big name is a great thing, and any show is improved by a big get. It can attract new listeners, and stir up activity on social media. Still, be intentional and thoughtful when booking them and don't invest too much time in something that may fall apart.

You won't usually get a chance to pre-interview a celebrity, but you don't really need one. The purpose of a pre-interview is to make sure the person can talk well, to gauge the extent of their knowledge of the topic and to collect information that might make the actual interview go smoothly.

The pre-interview shouldn't take more than 10 to 15 minutes. Try to ask a variety of questions, both specific and open-ended. You want to find out if the guest can speak off-the-cuff without stumbling, has energy, and can field questions that are off-topic. Ask for specific examples and stories. You want to be able to give the host some guidance on what makes the guest open up or laugh.

Do your research and choose four or five things that you want to know. Don't make a list of questions. Instead, ask yourself, "What do I want to know?" And don't try to recreate an answer they gave to some other reporter. It's highly unlikely that they'll repeat the same thing they've said before with the same authenticity and emotional power that they had the first time.

One of the most important things to remember when you're doing a pre-interview is that you don't want the guest to spill everything with you on the phone. You're trying to lead them up to the emotional line and stop just short of it. Neal Conan talked about this during the National Conference on Public Radio Talk Shows in 2002: "People you talk with about emotional kinds of stories tend to be people who are not used to being interviewed; the witness to the fire, whatever it is. If somebody's got an emotional story, make sure they don't spill it during the pre-interview. You have to tell these people who are doing the pre-interviews, don't let them have catharsis with you! I want them to have catharsis on the radio. They're only going to tell this story well once. I want the audience to hear it. Try to keep those reactions as fresh as you possibly can."

4. BROADCAST WRITING

Don't say the old lady screamed. Bring her on and let her scream.

-- Mark Twain

What I see most is people who have not organized their story so that it has a beginning, middle and an end. I think of a story like a trapeze act. You're holding onto this trapeze and you're about to jump off to the next one. And if the next one isn't there, you're going to fall.

The story is the same way. You're carrying the listener along on the trapeze, you jump from one conceptual swing in your piece... is the next handle going to be there for the listener to grab hold of it? And you have to explicitly address that in your story: how you get from the beginning, to the middle, to the end. And have it all make sense to someone who is NOT sitting there reading it, but who is probably only going to be able to hear it once.

-- Laura Bertran, former NPR Senior Editor

Writing for the ear is very different from writing for the eye. Most of us spend our lives learning to write for print, but very few learn how to write for broadcast. Even in journalism school, students are mostly trained to write prose and not dialogue. That means every person in radio, at some point, had to learn how to write in a new way.

The primary thing to keep in mind is that your audience has to absorb and retain a great deal of information using only their ears. If they don't understand something, they can't go back and re-read the sentence. Your writing should be brief, precise and engaging.

I've split this guide to writing into two sections: basics and not-so-basic. As with anything, these rules aren't hard and fast. But I don't recommend breaking them until you've learned how to use them. Robert Frost once said that writing poetry without rhythm and rhyme is like "playing tennis with the net down." Anyone can do it and no one wants to watch it. The same is true of broadcast writing. It needs structure.

THE BASICS

1. Write conversationally. Write as people would talk if they used proper grammar and complete sentences, and didn't run on and on and on. Journalists have a tendency to slip into "reporter-speak." The Poynter Institute for Media Studies maintains a list of things that only reporters say, like "laceration," "according to", "slain", and "lambaste." The point is, steer away from words and sentence constructions that are unnatural.

2. Don't put unfamiliar names or references in your lead. Remember that people have to understand what you're saying immediately. If they stop for a moment to figure out what you said, they're already missing what comes next.

3. Round off all of your numbers unless the exact amount is important (death tolls are always important - try not to use estimating language for deaths, as in "at least 400 people died" or "around 20 are dead." It comes off as insensitive.)

4. Spell out all numbers up to and including eleven. After that, you can write 43, 21, etc. But larger numbers should be written like this: "14-hundred" or "88-million". Also write "in the morning" instead of am and the same for pm.

5. Age always goes before a person's name and is hyphenated (14-year-old student Mike Hampton)

6. Include only one thought per sentence. You're writing for radio. You need short declarative sentences people can understand easily. Like these. Sometimes, if it's long enough, someone's title is a thought. So write, "Pam Stuart is the Director of the Office for Support and Coordination in the UN Department of Economic and Social Affairs." That's more than enough to take in. Let that be a complete sentence. Add a period and then start fresh with something else.

7. Use colors in your writing: red, green, indigo, violet, lemon yellow, and navy blue. Colors are a powerful stimulant to the imagination.

8. Intros should be short and direct. That means, don't give us a history of the segment. Don't try to foreshadow what the interview will be about, and don't include clips that are unrelated or unnecessary. If you have a clip in the intro, the rest of the copy should be short enough to keep the intro brief. Research tells us listeners will only pay attention to about 20 seconds of intro. You need to be in and then out and into the story.

9. Avoid passive voice. Here's an easy reminder: if you can insert "by zombies" after the verb, you're writing in passive voice. So here's a sentence in active voice: John Smith won the election. And here it is in passive voice: The election was won (by zombies) by John Smith. There are occasions when passive voice can be effective, particularly when the object is more important than the agent, as in "The White House was destroyed by fire." Passive voice can be a divisive subject among grammar enthusiasts, but I'd advise you to avoid it whenever possible. Instead of: A contract between PEPCO and city officials will be signed later today, try this: PEPCO and city officials will sign a contract later today.

10. Look for words that end in "-ing" and eliminate them if you can – Words that end in -ing are usually unnecessary. In casual conversation, no one says, "Strolling down Woodward, the officer encountered a group of teens". It's also best to avoid verb constructions with -ing. Instead of "Celeste will be hosting the show", write "Celeste will host the show" or "Celeste hosts the show."

11. Don't use subordinate clauses. They are great in print, but hard to understand in broadcasting. Look for the words "which" and "who," as they generally signal the presence of a subordinate clause. For example: "The congressman, who last year voted against increasing veterans' benefits, says the VA needs more funding." People don't use subordinate clauses when they talk.

12. No quotation marks or ellipses (the three dots used to indicate something missing) in your copy. That's print style. Those things are easily misinterpreted when you're reading. Write exactly what you want to be read. (i.e. - "President Obama said -QUOTE- quotation marks don't work in broadcast copy. -END QUOTE-")

13. Don't justify why we have certain guests. In other words, you don't need to say "reporter John Middleton joins us. He's covered this issue for years." If it's important, it will come out in the interview. Audiences have said they don't really care about those details. They assume if we have invited a specific guest, it's because they're qualified to talk about the issue.

14. Percentages/numbers - '50 percent' can also be described as 'half', '200 percent' are 'twice' or 'double'. Draw comparisons to translate information about size and/or distance. If, for example, you mention a building site is about the size of two football fields, listeners will visualize this better than if you describe the size in square meters or feet.

15. Choose strong verbs over adverbs. Instead of saying "he crawled out carefully," try writing "he slunk out."

You should also format your script with large margins, double spaced, with a font size 14 or larger. The point of this is to make the script easy to read. Be sure you do a mouth edit before handing it off to an editor or host. Say it out loud. If you can't say it, your host probably can't either. If you stumble over the copy, you should probably rewrite it.

Now, we'll move on to some more sophisticated principles of broadcast writing. But I'd recommend you master the above principles before moving on.

NOT-SO-BASICS

1. Write in short sentences. This is an extension and expansion of number 6 above. Think of it as small bites of information that the average listener won't choke on. Not "As it stands, state law prohibits squirrels from driving unless accompanied by a licensed chipmunk, although that could change when the legislature votes on the issue next week." Instead: "Squirrels can't drive

in this state unless they're supervised by a licensed chipmunk. The state legislature may change that next week."

2. Don't repeat yourself. That includes restating the same statistic from another angle or summarizing what a source is about to say in a clip.

3. Generally, the strength of your writing is in the story you're telling, not the language itself. Use adjectives only when they help the listener understand the story. Use adverbs only when they add to clarity. A successful story is not the one that elicits a response of "what a great writer!" but the one that makes people understand the issue, get a new perspective, think about it in a new way.

4. Surprise is essential. Not plot twists and shocks, but unexpected information, thoughts that shed a new light, perspectives that people haven't considered. If you're telling people exactly what they expect to hear, you're probably wasting air time.

5. Make your description a thought. Don't just add a list of adjectives before your noun. If you're describing a piece of art, don't say "large, colorful, gilt-framed painting" - say "The canvas is coated in thick smears of red, black and purple paint. It's the size of a ping pong table and is framed in gold."

6. Be sparing with humor. Do you use puns in regular life? If not, don't use them on the air. Humor is unlikely to translate when a host is reading someone else's line. The purpose of colloquialisms and witty comments is usually to make the show sound more human and authentic. If your host is reading something off the page that he would never say in real life, it's counterproductive. That doesn't mean you remove

cleverness from your writing--just the little jokes and puns.

7. Don't draw conclusions. Don't tell the listener what it is, tell them how you know it is so. Using the word "finally" is actually subjective. It implies you think it took too long, or were happy to see it happen. It's not neutral. Consider this sentence: "The demonstrators are protesting against pollution that will be caused by the new factory." Now, ask yourself, will the factory really pollute the environment or is this primarily the opinion of the environmentalists? Try this instead: "Protesters believe the new factory will be harmful to the environment."

8. Any audio you pull should clarify instead of confuse. Every so often, we get a clip that's hard to understand or requires a good amount of explanation that's not central to the focus of your segment. Don't pull clips just to pull clips.

9. Avoid vague terms that are so common in journalism, like "officials," "analysts," and "experts." Jonathan Kern calls them "meaningless attributions". His example is instead of writing, "Ford officials say they're coming out with a new hybrid car," say "Ford is coming out with a new hybrid car." NPR did an analysis of its content and found the word "officials" had been used more than 2,000 times in one year. Ombudsman Mark Memmott suggests we use specific titles in place of vague descriptors. He says, "The ubiquitous 'experts,' for example, might be 'biologists,' 'historians' or 'numismatists,' depending on their specialties."

6. THE INTERVIEW

The day before an interview, email or call the guest to confirm the details. Do it again on the day of the interview. When it's time for the segment, even though the host is in the studio, you still have responsibilities to perform.

I wrote earlier about what the host can and should do to make a guest feel at ease. All of that applies to the producers as well. You should use the same techniques to make the guest feel comfortable before you seat them in the studio.

When the guest arrives, or you get them on the phone, you should do whatever you can to put him at ease. Chat for a couple of minutes about his commute, his family, anything light. Don't talk to him about the subject of the interview; let the host broach the subject. As Neal Conan says, you want the guest's reactions to be as fresh as possible. Offer the guest some coffee or water, seat them comfortably and check his mic levels.

Now, give the guest an idea of how the interview works. Remind the guest to turn off their cell phone or leave it outside the studio. Explain the host will read an intro and then ask them some questions. Tell him he can relax, the host is just going to have a conversation with him.

This is a good time to gently coach your guest. Remind him that he should keep it brief and keep responses simple. He doesn't need to tell the listeners everything he knows about the topic; the goal is not to be encyclopedic. Tell them to let their passion for the subject shine through, because listeners respond to that kind of energy. And make sure you tell them that the host will try to break in, if necessary, and they should be on the lookout for efforts to ask a follow-up question or cut them short.

While the host is conducting the interview, listen carefully and stay connected through Google Chat or whatever chat client you use. You can fact check for the host in real time, cue up audio and music as needed, and remain prepared to supply whatever it takes to make the interview go smoothly.

7. EDIT

There's not much guidance I can give you on editing interviews. Why? Because that will ultimately be worked out with your editor and executive producer. But I can give you a couple of tips that may help.

First, make sure the finished piece has a beginning, middle and end. Even if it means you have to cut out your favorite bite, don't disrupt the storyline. If the guest took some time to warm up, then cut the top, move any essential information into the intro, and start where the guest became engaging and passionate.

Be careful what you choose to cut. In the book *Sound Reporting*, Scott Simon says "if he has asked a question that would occur to most listeners, he expects it to stay in the interview--even if a producer thinks the answer wasn't informative or substantial. 'The classic example to me years ago was when we were interviewing a young woman who was on her high school wrestling team. In those days, she was the only young woman on a high school varsity team who was competing against young men. And I asked what I think is the first question on almost everybody's mind, which is, 'Are your opponents sometimes reluctant to touch you because you're a girl?' And her answer to that was, 'No, I haven't noticed that.' So it didn't get in the edited version! And it sounded like we didn't ask it."

THE BASICS OF AUDIO

As a producer, you'll have to leave the studio to record audio in the field. Getting good audio is a science *and* an art. The science comes first and then, with work, the art. Here's a beginner's guide.

1. Bring the right equipment and check it before you leave! Get in the habit of running a checklist every time you're preparing to leave to gather sound.
   a. Do you have extra batteries?
   b. Plug in the recorder - does it turn on?
   c. Does it record?
   d. Do you have headphones? Windscreen for mic?
   e. Do you have mic cables and duct tape?
   f. Do you need a shotgun or an omnidirectional? Do you need more than one mic?

The best mic for crowd noise and ambient sound is an omnidirectional like the RE-50. It does well in quiet environments, but it will focus in on the loudest sound in the area. So it's not good for doing an interview with an individual in a crowd. The best mic for everything else is a unidirectional or shotgun. This type of mic focuses in on what it's pointed at. It almost always needs a windscreen. Many of them do not use phantom power and require a battery.

This excerpt from the website for "This American Life" explains why the show prefers unidirectional microphones: *We like shotgun mics because they give you a prettier sound for interviews with less room noise, and when you need to capture the sounds of machines clicking and cows mooing and all the other ambient audio that makes up a radio documentary, you can point at what you're trying to record and isolate it from the surrounding environment a bit. Occasionally in specialized situations we'll also use a wireless mic, which is a great thing to have but definitely not a necessity for a beginner. Ira recalls: "I bought my first wireless when I was 33.*

I'd worked in radio for 14 years without one. It was, no kidding, more expensive than the car I drove at the time, a pro Lectrosonics rig that cost me $1800."

Although you may choose to buy your own gear, most stations provide the essentials. I bought my own microphone and digital recorder for use on freelance assignments, but my kit bag with mic, Marantz digital recorder, XLR cords and batteries belonged to the newsroom.

2. Get a minimum of 30 seconds of ambient sound in every place you record. I get ambient sound both before I begin the interview and when I'm finished because the soundscape can change. If you move to another location or room, get more ambient sound. And identify the location in the audio, so it can't get lost. You can never have too much ambient sound, but you can easily have too little. In fact, most people get too little. Make sure there is no music playing anywhere in the background. You can't cut audio if music is playing. If you're in a gallery or store where there's background music, try to move the person away from it, then go get ambient sound of the room that you can add in later to help smooth edits.

There is a difference between ambient sound that you may need to fade into and out of a cut and the ambient sound that you will feature in a piece. The first type will most likely never be heard alone and you need, as I mentioned, at least 30 secs of it. But if you're at a skate park, concert, dairy farm, anywhere the sound of the place will be heard in isolation and at full volume at some point, then you need several minutes of the sound. Stop walking to get it unless you want the effect of moving through the environment and you don't mind hearing footsteps.

3. Listen back to the ambient sound to make sure the equipment is functioning properly. If there's a short in the cable, you could record the entire interview without knowing that it's unusable. So don't skip this step.

4. Don't use pause on the recorder. If you do, you will inevitably forget to take it off pause at some point and then get to the end of an interview only to discover that you weren't recording. So don't use it at all. Either the recorder is on or off. Turn the recorder on, make sure you see the time counter going up to show it's recording.

5. Have each person you interview say their name and title on the recording before you start the interview.

6. Mic placement - The mic needs to be about a fist length away from the person's mouth, which is 3-5 inches. DO NOT EVER LET THE GUEST TOUCH THE MIC! I generally angle the mic very slightly away from their mouth so expelled breath and p-pops don't ruin the sound, but you should be listening closely on your headphones and adjusting as needed. I generally ask a filler question at the start so I can adjust the mic and the levels. You can fix low volume but there's nothing you can do about sound that's clipping (i.e., too loud). It's ruined.

7. Have the guest describe what they're talking about and point to it, if possible. You'll want to record the guest saying things like, "That's the house, there, where I saw the SWAT team burst through the door." There's a different quality to the interview when the guest is describing what they see. It brings the listener directly into the scene.

8. Put your back to the noise and move away from it. A common trick when recording in a windy or noisy place is to do the interview inside your car with the windows open. Don't rush because without good sound, you might as well not have done the interview at all.

9. Get in the habit of nodding and smiling or frowning. Non-verbal communication is your friend. You want to respond to the guest so they feel like they're having a conversation with a human being, but you don't want to say "uh-huh" or "yeah" or "oh no" and ruin your bite. Learn how to be a human emoticon.

10. Using your/the guest's smartphone. To do this, your guest will need access to two phones: the phone they will talk into and the phone that will record their voice. Most smartphones have a voice recording app, like the VoiceMemo on the iPhone. Have them create a test recording and listen back so they know how far to hold the phone's mic from their mouths. Remind them to keep that hand steady and try not to move their head too much while recording. Make sure to tell them when to begin recording and when to stop. Then, have the guest transfer the file, using SoundCloud or weTransfer or whatever method you choose.

REPORTER'S "GO BAG" CHECKLIST

THE ESSENTIALS
- Lightweight but sturdy bag
- Smartphone
- Charging cord
- External charger
- Notebook + pens

KEEP IT TOGETHER
- Store your checklist with your bag
- Designate a place for each item
- Recharge + repack as soon as you get home
- Experiment with apps (like the ones below)
- Try out new apps at home, not in the field

FOR VISUALS
- DSLR camera or smartphone with upgraded camera + video apps
- Mobile lenses, mobile tripod

FOR AUDIO
- Over-the-ear headphones with a splitter
- Handheld audio recorder or free recording app
- Mobile-friendly external microphone

LEAVE BEHIND
- Food + makeup that could end up in your gear
- Your laptop, if possible

Improve your video with the MOVIEPRO app or broadcast standups from the field with USTREAM

Use the IRIG app to connect an external mic or record with AUDIOBOOM to upload to the web

Take better pics with Camera Awesome for Android or CAMERA+ for iPhone

Back up your files with DROPBOX, and share with the world via TWITTER, FACEBOOK + INSTAGRAM apps

Source: Interviews with Amara Aguilar (@amara_media) + Doug Mitchell (@nextgenradio), who train young journalists to tell compelling stories for public media through the #nextgenradio program.

ETHICS

By far, the most important ethical responsibility you assume as a journalist is accuracy. Facts should be checked and double-checked before they are published or broadcast. Below is a handy checklist adapted from a guide created by the Detroit Free Press through the work of its accuracy and credibility committee. I've edited it to be more relevant for broadcast journalists.

REPORTER CHECKLIST
1. Have you double-checked all names, titles and places mentioned in your story?
2. Are the quotes accurate and properly attributed? Have you fully captured what
each person meant?
3. Is this story fair? Who or what might be missing from the story? Have they
been called and given a chance to talk?
4. Have you run spell check and checked the math?

EDITOR CHECKLIST
1. Did the reporter double-check all names, titles and places mentioned in this
story?
2. Are the quotes accurate and properly attributed? Have we fully captured what
each person meant?
3. Is the story fair? Who or what might be missing from the story? Is the lede or
nut graph sufficiently supported?
4. Are there visual elements that could be used on the website? Have you heard the completed piece?
5. Are the background and context complete enough to tell listeners why the story
is relevant?
6. Did the reporter sign off on changes made in the story?

And here is the Code of Ethics from the Society of Professional Journalists. This is used as a basis for ethics policies at many stations.

PREAMBLE
Members of the Society of Professional Journalists believe that public enlightenment is the forerunner of justice and the foundation of democracy. The duty of the journalist is to further those ends by seeking truth and providing a fair and comprehensive account of events and issues. Conscientious journalists from all media and specialties strive to serve the public with thoroughness and honesty. Professional integrity is the cornerstone of a journalist's credibility.
Members of the Society share a dedication to ethical behavior and adopt this code to declare the Society's principles and standards of practice.

SEEK TRUTH AND REPORT IT
Journalists should be honest, fair and courageous in gathering, reporting and interpreting information.
Journalists should:
- Test the accuracy of information from all sources and exercise care to avoid inadvertent error. Deliberate distortion is never permissible.
- Diligently seek out subjects of news stories to give them the opportunity to respond to allegations of wrongdoing.
- Identify sources whenever feasible. The public is entitled to as much information
  as possible on sources' reliability.
- Always question sources' motives before promising anonymity. Clarify conditions attached to any promise made in exchange for information. Keep promises.
- Make certain that headlines, news teases and promotional material, photos, video, audio, graphics, sound bites and quotations do not misrepresent. They should not oversimplify or highlight incidents out of context.

- Never distort the content of news photos or video. Image enhancement for technical clarity is always permissible. Label montages and photo illustrations.
- Avoid misleading re-enactments or staged news events. If re-enactment is necessary to tell a story, label it.
- Avoid undercover or other surreptitious methods of gathering information except when traditional open methods will not yield information vital to the public. Use of such methods should be explained as part of the story.
- Never plagiarize.
- Tell the story of the diversity and magnitude of the human experience boldly,
  even when it is unpopular to do so.
- Examine their own cultural values and avoid imposing those values on others.
- Avoid stereotyping by race, gender, age, religion, ethnicity, geography, sexual orientation, disability, physical appearance or social status.
- Support the open exchange of views, even views they find repugnant.
- Give voice to the voiceless; official and unofficial sources of information can be equally valid.
- Distinguish between advocacy and news reporting. Analysis and commentary should be labeled and not misrepresent fact or context.
- Distinguish news from advertising and shun hybrids that blur the lines between the two.
- Recognize a special obligation to ensure that the public's business is conducted in the open and that government records are open to inspection.

MINIMIZE HARM
Ethical journalists treat sources, subjects and colleagues as human beings deserving of respect. Journalists should:
- Show compassion for those who may be affected adversely by news coverage.

- Use special sensitivity when dealing with children and inexperienced sources or subjects.
- Be sensitive when seeking or using interviews or photographs of those affected by tragedy or grief:
- Recognize that gathering and reporting information may cause harm or discomfort.
- Pursuing the news is not a license for arrogance.
- Recognize that private people have a greater right to control information about themselves than do public officials and others who seek power, influence or attention.
- Only an overriding public need can justify intrusion into anyone's privacy.
- Show good taste. Avoid pandering to lurid curiosity.
- Be cautious about identifying juvenile suspects or victims of sex crimes.
- Be judicious about naming criminal suspects before the formal filing of charges.
- Balance a criminal suspect's fair trial rights with the public's right to be informed.

ACT INDEPENDENTLY

Journalists should be free of obligation to any interest other than the public's right to know. Journalists should:

- Avoid conflicts of interest, real or perceived.
- Remain free of associations and activities that may compromise integrity or damage credibility.
- Refuse gifts, favors, fees, free travel and special treatment, and shun secondary employment, political involvement, public office and service in community organizations if they compromise journalistic integrity.
- Disclose unavoidable conflicts.
- Be vigilant and courageous about holding those with power accountable.
- Deny favored treatment to advertisers and special interests and resist their pressure to influence news coverage.
- Be wary of sources offering information for favors or money; avoid bidding for news.

BE ACCOUNTABLE

Journalists are accountable to their readers, listeners, viewers and
each other. Journalists should:

- Clarify and explain news coverage and invite dialogue with the public over journalistic conduct.
- Encourage the public to voice grievances against the news media.
- Admit mistakes and correct them promptly.
- Expose unethical practices of journalists and the news media.
- Abide by the same high standards to which they hold others.

Check out NPR's Code of Ethics online as well.

You can use these documents as a guide to create a code of ethics that works for your team. Remember to include guidelines on social media.

FINAL THOUGHTS

A new show is like a new baby. The first two years will exhaust you and try your spirit, but you know it's worth it. At two and a half, things start to settle in and you begin to really enjoy yourself.

Your show will most likely not be an instant hit, and that's okay. While your audience is relatively small, you have the chance to experiment and make mistakes in front of a smaller crowd. Remember, NPR rejected both *Prairie Home Companion* and *This American Life*. It took the *Car Talk* guys nine years to get their own show. So, be patient and prepare for the long haul.

I've included a couple other essays that I've written on radio news topics, including why you shouldn't argue with your guests (looking at you, Don Lemon) and why you shouldn't interview children soon after a tragedy occurs. But there is a lot of incredible source material out there that I've found helpful, so spend some time looking around at the materials provided.

Remember, journalists are like musicians. We should continue training for the rest of our lives. Don't stagnate. Grow. There is always training available and people willing to be a mentor.

In the meantime, good luck with your show. I wish you crystal clear audio signals, verified breaking news sources, and celebrities who will break down into tears when you mention their mothers. Enjoy the process!

LEXICON

Actualities – Also known as a "sound bite," this is a clip of someone making a comment that's used in a report

Anchor - Someone who fills in breaks on the local version of a network show (i.e., local anchor of *Morning Edition*)

Cut-and-Copy – A spot that includes an actuality.

CR - Control room

Downcut – Cutting off the end of an audio clip or story. The opposite of an upcut.

Forward promote – A line that tells audiences about an upcoming segment, ex. "We'll talk to a woman who found her dog six years after losing it, but first..."

IQ – Stands for "in cue", or the first few words of an actuality

ISDN – This stands for Integrated Services for Digital Network. It's a completely digital telecommunications network. When connected, the sound is clean and high quality and usually sounds as though the people connected are in the same room together.

Host - Someone who holds down their own show

Tease - A short promo for what's coming up in a show, usually placed just before a break

Two-way - An interview with two people, a host and a guest

MOS – This is an acronym for "man on the street." It refers to short interviews done with people walking around a certain area.

OQ – Stands for "out cue", or the final few words of an actuality

Outro - A short paragraph (usually one or two sentences) that the anchor reads after an interview or feature or other segment. It generally includes the name of the reporter or the guests, plus basic information about an upcoming event, the name of the book that the author wrote, etc. For example, "Harriet Dexter is the author of 'Skateboarding in Tibet.' She'll speak and read from her book tonight at the Moonshine Bookstore at 7pm. Harriet, thank you.")

Peg - An event that brings a particular issue into the news on a specific day. In other words, the election is the peg for talking about voting rights.

Slug - The title of your segment, short enough to be saved as a data file and web page

Spot - A short news report, generally used in a headline break. Spots are usually 0:45, but certainly no more than a minute long

TRT – Stands for "total run time." It is the total length of a specific actuality or story or show or whatever audio you're measuring.

Upcut – Clipping the beginning of an audio clip or story. The opposite of downcut.

Vox - A shortening of the phrase "vox populi", meaning "voice of the people". Vox is a collection of short hits of tape from people you spoke to about a particular subject. If we did it for a newspaper, it would be called a survey.

ADDITIONAL MATERIAL

HOW TO GET YOUR FIRST JOB IN RADIO

First and foremost, ask for help. As I prepared to write this section, I posted the question in the Facebook group called "Public Media Journalists." I asked, "What advice would you give someone on how to get their first job in radio?" Within 24 hours, I had two pages of responses. Bradley George, the *Morning Edition* anchor at Georgia Public Broadcasting said, "If you're new to the business and feeling discouraged, there's someone out there who is willing to help you." And Katie Colaneri of StateImpact Pennsylvania wrote, you should "network like crazy. I made a former public radio reporter-turned-PR flak have coffee with me to talk about the biz. He introduced me to Doug Doyle at WBGO and the rest is history."

There is no one ideal path to your first job. I got into radio purely by chance and Adam Ragusea, host of the podcast "The Pub," says he "stumbled bass-ackward" into his first job. Bob Edwards, Peabody award-winning former host of *Morning Edition* tells this story: "I was carefully watching the morning drive DJ at WHEL in New Albany, Indiana, in 1968. I was 21 and hoping for substitute work. The police arrived and arrested the DJ for non-support. I finished his shift."

So, lightning can and does strike, but there are also proven techniques to get your foot in the door.

> 1.   Create content – Don't wait for someone to give you a job or assign a story. The way to become a reporter is to report on something. If you don't have professional equipment, take your smartphone and gather audio.

Write your story, record interviews and your tracks and then use an audio editor (Audacity is free in its basic form) to create your piece. To apply for either a job or internship, you'll want to have a demo that includes a variety of pieces: a feature, a spot and a vox piece, for example. So, go out there and create them! You can even create your own podcast.

Jed Mann is now a reporter with *Marketplace* in California, but he was once a rookie looking for his first job. He says, "I was up for a job at NPR a few years ago – back before I had gotten even my first radio reporting job – and the editor who was hiring told me I was considered a [viable] candidate because I had actual clips to share." Later, Jed says he used the same strategy to get a job at a public radio station in Los Angeles: "I identified a show [at KPCC] that needed freelance content, and I hit them up repeatedly. When a fill-in reporting position at the station opened up, the people there knew I could write, edit and produce."

2.   Take whatever opening is available. Take an internship, find a fellowship, work: one journalist said his first job in radio was as a janitor at a station. This was, far and away, the most common piece of advice from seasoned professionals: don't be picky about your first gig. Do college radio, volunteer at a local community station, take even short-term positions if that's what is available.

It's best, if possible, to start this process while you're still in school. Granted, not everyone has the financial means to take an unpaid internship. If you do, make good use of your summers and free time.

Keep an open mind about every opportunity. Reporter Scott Gurian of WNYC tells this story about what he did early in his career when he needed a job: "I applied for every radio job I saw (for which I was qualified), literally from Bethel, Alaska to Dili, East Timor. I ended up getting a job offer at a station in Norman, Oklahoma... I remember telling my mom that Norman sounded like the most boring place on the face of the planet, but in retrospect, it ended up being an excellent decision, as I was hired to be News Director at the tender age of 24!... I got to host my own show, make occasional TV appearances, anchor gubernatorial candidate debates and win a bunch of awards, all experiences and opportunities that would have taken many more years to achieve at most larger stations in larger cities! It was a great way to jumpstart my career."

I, too, got my start at a smaller station in Flagstaff, Arizona. When the staff is small, you learn how to do all kinds of things, like run your own board and set up town hall events. At a large station like WNYC or WHYY, you won't get the diversity of training that you will in Norman or Flagstaff. Start small.

3.   Once you get a foot in the door, don't put it in your mouth. That is to say, when someone gives you a shot, make it count. Show up on time, meet your deadlines, do your best work and be ready to learn. Recommendations are the job hunter's most valuable currency, so be respectful and mature and honest and open to correction.

While I was at WDET in Detroit, we had an intern who was rude to all of the staff members except the Assistant News Director. Why? Because she planned to use only his name as a reference on her resume. But when she applied for a position, the person doing the hiring was a good friend of mine. He called and asked me about her and I told him the truth: she was disrespectful and argumentative. She didn't get the job. Broadcasting is a small world. Everyone you work with is a possible reference, not just the ones you choose to list on your application.

Adam Ragusea of "The Pub" says he got good at radio because he entered the profession with an open mind and nothing to prove. "From the age of 10 or 12," he says, "I was dead-set on being a composer. I had a very clear end goal in mind and it caused me to lose sight of the incremental steps that were necessary to achieving that goal. I wouldn't do my counterpoint homework because I wanted to work on my orchestra piece, for example.

When I stumbled into my first job at a radio station, I had no expectations or goals. It was just a job. As a result, I focused on doing every menial task that was before me as well as I could, instead of being preoccupied with getting the radio job I 'really wanted'. I did the job I had well, and that led to incrementally greater opportunities, Eventually, I landed in the perfect job that I never knew I was working toward. The point is, get into the system any way you can, even if it's not your ideal position. Do it well and have faith that your good work will be rewarded." It may take a while.

4.   Find a mentor (or two). As I mentioned above, most people in this industry are more than happy to offer advice and assistance when they can. Don't wait for someone to offer guidance, ask for it. Send your feature to someone you admire and ask them to critique it.

When I was first starting out, I had the great good fortune to learn under Cindy Carpien. Cindy was one of NPR's founding mothers and she is as experienced and smart as she is generous with her time. I did everything that she said, because I wasn't in a position to question what she was telling me. When I had a question, I asked. When I thought I did well, I asked her if she agreed. When I screwed up, I asked her what went wrong. Whatever success I've had in broadcasting can be traced directly back to the incredible guidance I received while working with Cindy in Flagstaff. So, find a mentor and then listen to him or her. You have to learn the rules before you can break them.

5.   Be persistent. Willis Kern of WGLT in Illinois says, "Don't take no for an answer," and that sentiment was echoed by several other professionals. Obviously, you can take this too far. Don't let persistence become harassment. However, you can get a lot of "nos" before you finally get a "yes." Stick with it. Brian Bull of WCPN says, "Be gracious if declined, welcome feedback and advice afterwards."

I got a lengthy response from Benny Becker, who works as a reporter and producer at WMMT in Kentucky. He spent two years working and maneuvering his way from unpaid college radio intern to full-time reporter/producer and he's learned a lot in the process:

My biggest takeaway is that nobody wants to pay you while they're teaching you the basic skills, or really, until you've already proven that you can be a critical and contributing team member.

Usually that means you have to work for free or peanuts. If you're committed to living in a particular place, it's good to get involved with as much as you can, time allowing. If not, there's more opportunity in more obscure places.

Smaller and younger outfits give more opportunity to do your own pieces, but bigger and more professional outlets (like a local NPR affiliate) will usually have you working with more experienced and detail-oriented editors and that's really important for learning. I think if you're working somewhere unpaid for a full year, that's not a good sign. If you want to get paid to work at that place, you should be able to make yourself a necessary part of the daily operations by then.

This isn't a healthy way for our industry to find new talent, by the way. Because most people start out in unpaid positions, lots of young journalists are priced out of the talent pool. But if you are able to afford it, remember that working for a year without pay is still cheaper than going to graduate school.

Networking is critical. If you can afford to attend a conference like Third Coast, you're not guaranteed to get a job but it's often a great chance to scope out what's happening and who's hiring. Sometimes people there are looking for help (that's how I got my first full-time gig and that turned into my first paid full-time gig after a few months).

Also, mastering the hard skills will go a long way toward making you a better candidate. Know how to get a clean recording, how to edit audio, and how to handle a sound board.

Lastly, a few random pieces of advice: Don't go away on holidays because that's when you're most likely to get a chance to fill in for someone. Be very careful when you write your cover letter. This is an industry filled with good writers and some news directors will throw your application away if they see typos or spelling errors. Use names, instead of sending letters to unnamed news directors at stations.

And one final piece of advice: listen. Listen to other people's work. Take note of what you like and what you don't. Be an active and critical audience. "Listen to the radio you want to be part of," says Sue Stephens of Northern Public Radio, "Listen to the radio you hate. If you want to be a good speller, read a lot. If you want to be a good broadcaster, listen all the time."

As a broadcaster, your training will never be complete. Keep your eyes open for opportunities to learn and work, and learn whatever someone is willing to teach you. When those opportunities come (and they will), do your best work.

ARGUING WITH GUESTS DOESN'T MAKE YOU A BETTER INTERVIEWER

I want to address the coverage of 2013 government shutdown using a few videos. Let's begin with this skit from the folks at Jimmy Kimmel Live. I acknowledge that this video was exploited for its comedic value and the polling is hardly scientific here. Still, polls consistently show that most Americans approve of the provisions in the Affordable Care Act, even if they respond negatively to the name "Obamacare."

What does this have to do with the budget that keeps the government running? ABSOLUTELY NOTHING! The President has said, and he is correct in doing so, that the shutdown of the government doesn't affect the rollout of the ACA one iota. Exchanges opened on Tuesday and, in typical government fashion, were unable to handle the number of visitors at the website. Anyone who's ever been to a DMV was probably not surprised that the government's health care portal was crowded, irritating and slow.

Back to the issue at hand, though: the only reason that we are talking about the ACA in connection with the budget is because House Republicans decided to tie the delay or defunding of the law to the continued operation of the government. That's not a partisan talking point; that's simply the truth. Dan Froomkin writes that "the political media's aversion to doing anything that might be seen as taking sides — combined with its obsession with process — led them to actively obscure the truth in their coverage of the votes. If you did not already know what this was all about, reading the news would not help you understand." He goes on to say that "the shutdown is not generalized dysfunction or gridlock or stalemate. It is aberrational behavior by a political party that is willing to take extreme and potentially damaging action to get its way. And by not calling it what it is, the political press is enabling it. We need a more fearless media."

Responding to strong criticism like this and from public anger over both the shutdown and the behavior of our elected representatives, some journalists have decided to get tougher. For the most part, it has not gone well. Here's Carol Costello with Rep. Todd Rokita (R-IN) on CNN. I applaud Costello's attempt to hold Rokita accountable, but she wasn't prepared to do so. Rokita says several incorrect things and skews the facts fairly openly. Costello should have corrected them instead of arguing.

He says they've sent many proposals to the Senate, Costello should have said that all of those proposals include provisions for defunding or delaying the ACA. Ask him if he supports a clean CR. When an anchor argues with a guest, it supports the idea that there are always two sides to everything, that absolutely nothing in politics can be established as fact. Don't argue. Just counter untruths with truths and get a response.

Here's another train wreck. Thomas Roberts is talking to RNC Chair Reince Priebus about the shutdown. And again, Roberts chooses to argue with Priebus. It becomes a contest in who can be heard above the other and by the end, it's almost unwatchable. Here, I'm less concerned about facts and that's because Reince Priebus is the Chair of the RNC. His job, quite literally, is to represent the party line. You expect talking points from him, and that's what Roberts got. It's a bit asinine to then argue that he's only giving you talking points.

Finally, here's a link to the TV interview that really shows you how to do this right:

Oh, sorry. I couldn't find one.

INTERVIEWING KIDS

The Golden Rule:

"Do unto other people's kids as you would have them do unto your kids." (From participants of "Children, Families, and Social Issues Seminar"-The Poynter Institute 1998)

December 14, 2012, was a tough day for the nation, but it was excruciating for the families of Sandy Hook Elementary School. 28 people are dead who were alive on Thursday, including 20 young children. That kind of loss is unimaginable, unnecessary, and unforgivable. But the number of victims is much higher than 28. As President Obama pointed out, "Our hearts are broken for the parents of the survivors as well, for as blessed as they are to have their children home tonight, they know that their children's innocence has been torn away from them too early, and there are no words that will ease their pain."

As the police were gathering the terrified kids and rushing them out of the building, the officers told the kids to close their eyes so they wouldn't see the blood and the bodies. It was a small thing, but if it prevented the kids from seeing something they wouldn't ever be able to forget, it was worth it. And that makes it one hundred times more despicable that when the children emerged from the building, traumatized and confused, they were met by reporters and photographers snapping pictures and shoving microphones and cameras in their faces.

I eventually turned the TV off because I couldn't bear to watch these kids and their parents being questioned. One reporter said to a child, "You weren't scared, were you?" Of course the kid was scared and how dare you, in any way, imply that he shouldn't have been.

Is there evidence that being questioned by reporters increases trauma for young kids? How about the personal experience of blogger Kim Simon, who was 14 when her friend was murdered at school? She says she remembers very little about what happened except, "YOU were there. YOU, with your enormous video cameras. YOU, with your microphones poking into the bubble of grief that grew bigger as we waited for our parents to find us. YOU, with your horrible questions about what had happened, had we known Mike, had we seen anything? No parents there yet, just children. No teachers, just children. **And you.**"

There is no journalistic value in the information an 8-year-old gives you when he or she has just gone through a horrifying experience, but there is a great deal of harm that you can do to both the child and the parents. What they say in the moment while still confused and hurt may be regretted at a later time. The Central Union for Child Welfare has this advice for reporters: "Children are also more vulnerable to publicity than adults, as children are not necessarily capable of evaluating their own privacy or knowing what should be kept secret about their own lives or the lives of those close to them. Nor are they necessarily capable of evaluating the effect of what they say on their own lives and those around them."

I assume that all of the reporters got permission from the parents to conduct these interviews but I don't think that makes a bit of difference. In a situation like that, where the parents are likely in a state of shock as well, the only person who is thinking clearly and making reasonable decisions is probably the reporter. So it is the journalist's responsibility to choose not to interview those suffering families.

These kids just got a terrifying lesson in how little the world can protect them if someone is determined to do them harm; the last thing they need is to then be exploited by professional journalists who are hoping to get every last ghastly detail. Asking a grade school kid to relive the moment when bullets were flying by his head does not add to my understanding of the situation at all. It's not useful information for me, it's voyeurism of the worst and most exploitative kind.

As James Poniewozik wrote at Time.com: "Reporting tragedy is terrible business, awful and necessary. Unspeakable things have happened, and it's a journalist's job to find out about them and tell the world… But there are much better ways to do this."

So yes, please, turn away the cameras. Better yet, turn them off until you've moved away from the children. We are professionals. We should do our job professionally and thoroughly, but we must also do it ethically. There should be a higher standard than "juiciest soundbyte, damn the cost." And that standard should always protect the most vulnerable among us.

ACKNOWLEDGEMENTS

This guide draws on the wisdom of many experienced, talented journalists. These people gave freely of their time and knowledge and their input was invaluable. They are: Jamila Bey, Cindy Carpien, Alex Cohen, Jeff Hansen, Steve Inskeep, Jay Kernis, Al Letson, Michel Martin, Rachel Martin, Ellen McDonnell, Irene Noguchi, Susan Stamberg, and Carline Watson.

This guide also owes a great deal to the many people who've trained me through the years, including (but not limited to) David Candow, Lester Graham, Valerie Kahler, Doug Mitchell, Harvey Ovshinsky, and Jerome Vaughn. I also want to acknowledge the many great fellowships I've had the privilege of participating in: the USC Annenberg/Getty Arts Fellowship, the fellowship with National Native News, the Institute for Journalism and Natural Resources, the Candow workshops sponsored by The Environment Report, and the many one- or two-day workshops and training programs and webinars offered through Poynter and Knight. Every bit of training helps.

A big thank you to the stations/networks that have employed me and helped me develop: KNAU in Flagstaff, WDET in Detroit, NPR, PRI, WNYC and Georgia Public Broadcasting.

Thanks to Dr. Lisa Wong, who gave me the title for the book.

A hearty thanks to my intrepid editor, Don Smith. He gave his time and knowledge freely and unsparingly. He probably removed several dozen mentions of "tape" and more than a hundred "thats."

And a special thanks to my son, Grant Headlee, who was my first editor and most critical reader ("OMG, Mom, did someone steal your commas? Should I call the cops?" and "Congratulations, you've successfully clunked up this saying more than it has ever been clunked up before. Mom, who would ever say it like that?")

www.ingramcontent.com/pod-product-compliance
Lightning Source LLC
Chambersburg PA
CBHW072046280526
45788CB00006B/2206